The Best of Casual Mediterranean Cooking

TAVERNA

SUNSET BOOKS
President and Publisher: Susan J. Maruyama
Director, Sales and Marketing: Richard A. Smeby
Production Director: Lory Day
Director, New Business: Kenneth Winchester
Editorial Director: Robert A. Doyle

SUNSET PUBLISHING CORPORATION
Chairman: Jim Nelson
President and Chief Executive Officer: Stephen J. Seabolt
Chief Financial Officer: James E. Mitchell
Publisher: Anthony P. Glaves
Circulation Director: Robert I. Gursha
Director of Finance: Larry Diamond
Vice President, Manufacturing: Lorinda R. Reichert
Editor, *Sunset Magazine:* William R. Marken

Produced by
WELDON OWEN INC.
President: John Owen
Vice President and Publisher: Wendely Harvey
Vice President and CFO: Richard VanOosterhout
Managing Editor: Lisa Chaney Atwood
Consulting Editor: Norman Kolpas
Copy Editor: Sharon Silva
Design: Patty Hill
Production Director: Stephanie Sherman
Production Coordinator: Tarji Mickelson
Production Editor: Janique Gascoigne
Editorial Assistant: Sarah Lemas
Co-Editions Director: Derek Barton
Food Photography: Peter Johnson
Assistant Food Photographer: Dal Harper
Food Stylist: Janice Baker
Assistant Food Stylist: Liz Nolan
Half-Title Illustration: Martha Anne Booth
Chapter Opener Illustrations: Ed Miller
Glossary Illustrations: Alice Harth

Production by Kyodo Printing Co.
(S'pore) Pte Ltd
Printed in Singapore

First Printing 1996
10 9 8 7 6 5 4 3 2 1

ISBN 0-376-02040-7
Library of Congress Catalog Card Number: 95-072206

A Note on Weights and Measures:
All recipes include customary U.S. and metric measurements.
Metric conversions are based on a standard developed for these
books and have been rounded off. Actual weights may vary.

A Note on Language:
For Greek words transliterated into the Roman alphabet, we
have used common spellings that make phonetic pronunciation
the simplest. In the case of Turkish, we have not included the
special diacritical marks that indicate pronunciation.

The Best of Casual Mediterranean Cooking

TAVERNA

by Joyce Goldstein

Contents

Introduction 7

Beverages 10
Fried Almonds 11

❧

BASIC RECIPES
Garlic-Potato Sauce 12
Yogurt-Cucumber Sauce 13
Tomato-Nut Sauce 14
Chili Pepper Sauce 15
Marinated Olives 15

Appetizers 17

Garlic Shrimp 18
Zucchini Fritters 21
Potato Omelet 22
Salt Cod Fritters 25
Stuffed Grape Leaves 26
Fried Cheese 29
Fried Mussels
with Nut Sauce 30
Grilled Eggplant Salad 33
Lamb Pizza 34
Cheese-Filled Pastries 37
Spinach Filo Pie 38

Soups and Vegetables 41

Chilled Tomato Soup 42
Bread Soup with Cilantro, Garlic
and Poached Egg 45
"Green" Soup
with Kale and Potatoes 46
Fish Soup 49
Meatball Soup
with Egg and Lemon 50
Greek Salad 53
Spinach with Raisins
and Pine Nuts 54
Sautéed Mushrooms
with Garlic 57
Stuffed Eggplant 58
City-Style Braised Artichokes 61
Rice Pilaf with Pine Nuts
and Currants 62
Eggplant and Tomato Pilaf 65

Fish and Shellfish 67

Stewed Clams with Sausage,
Ham and Tomatoes 68

Shrimp with Tomatoes,
Oregano and Feta 71

Fish in Grape Leaves 72

Gratin of Salt Cod
and Potatoes 75

Grilled Swordfish Kebabs 76

Fish in Almond Sauce 79

Stuffed Squid 80

Trout Wrapped in Ham 83

Paella 84

Poultry and Meat 87

Grilled Chicken Kebabs 88

Chicken with Eggplant,
Peppers and Tomatoes 91

Roast Chicken
with Oregano and Lemon 92

Sausage and Green
Pepper Ragout 95

Grilled Meatballs 96

Braised Pork with Quinces 99

Lamb Stew with Artichokes 100

Baked Lamb and Eggplant 103

Grilled Lamb on Skewers 104

Roast Leg of Lamb
with Yogurt 107

Pork Ragout with Sweet Red
Peppers and Lemon 108

Desserts 111

Cream-Filled Apricots 112

Rice Pudding 115

Sweet Cheese Tarts
from Santorini 116

Figs Stuffed with
Chocolate and Almonds 119

Baklava 120

Caramelized Orange Custard 123

❧

GLOSSARY 124

INDEX 128

Introduction

A well-worn bar, rough-hewn wooden tables, platters of steaming food, voices raised in spirited conversation, the clink of glasses, perhaps the bowing of a fiddler. These are the sights and sounds of a Mediterranean taverna, a kind of community social center that offers food, drink and friendship in equally generous portions.

A taverna can be a raucous sportsbar on a boat-lined harbor, the sole eating establishment in the central square of a white-washed village or a clubby hangout on a side street in a bustling big city. The menu specializes in local fare, from small plates ideal for accompanying the local wines and liquors to hearty soups, simmering stews and fragrant grilled meats. The staff is often small, sometimes only a cook and waiter, and the informal atmosphere is invariably warm and welcoming.

This casual setting draws shop clerks and students, bank presidents and fishermen, a family wedding party and a workingmen's card game. In other words, a taverna is a natural gathering place for all who enjoy rustic meals in friendly surroundings.

Taverna History

Taverna is a Greek word taken from the Latin *taberna,* or "tavern." Originally it was a place where Greek men passed the time drinking ouzo or wine and talking about daily life—a cross of sorts between a bar and a community living room. Gradually its role expanded, until today the Greek taverna has come to describe an informal establishment that offers both a place to talk and drink with friends and an affordable destination for those seeking home cooking away from home.

Although taverna is the Greek term for this informal dining spot, the type of rustic, country food that these establishments traditionally serve is available in several similar eateries across the Mediterranean. The following pages will explore the Greek taverna and its counterparts in a trio of equally temperate countries: Turkey, Portugal and Spain. Like the Greek taverna, restaurants in these countries offer both a no-frills approach to cooking and a casual environment in which to enjoy the sun-kissed fare of the Mediterranean and its surrounding regions.

In Turkey, this everyday restaurant is known as a *lokanta* (derived from the Italian *locanda* or "inn") or *meyhane,* and along its Aegean coast as a taverna. In Portugal, which boasts a Mediterranean spirit although not a Mediterranean coast, there is the *tasca,* an unassuming operation offering wine and a few simple dishes. And in Spain, people frequent a *taberna, tasca* or *tapas* bar, where the country's famed *tapas* and other modest fare are commonly paired with local wines.

The Taverna Experience

The word *taverna* conjures up a host of images that reach beyond Greece's national borders, so here it stands not only for the venerable Greek institution that it names, but also for the other tavernalike restaurants—the *lokanta, tasca* and *taberna*—that are explored in these pages.

Inside a taverna, animated conversations are an integral part of the scene. Drinking, smoking and waving of newspapers to make a point are age-old social customs. The owner is usually present, working at the bar or presiding over the cash register. Or perhaps he or she is toiling in the kitchen, stopping only to bark out a word to a waiter that a dish is ready. This is no hushed temple of cuisine, no recipient of stars in a food guide. It is a rustic place of and for the people who live nearby, a hangout where locals dine on food cooked by a neighbor.

Taverna cooks have seldom studied at a culinary institute. Instead, they are more often than not the wife or sister, mother or brother of the owner, and they draw upon long-cherished family recipes. Their kitchen is usually a small jerry-rigged alcove carved into the back

of the room or set in a corner. A large charcoal grill or brick oven, set up outside the taverna, is used for cooking fresh meat and fish under the open sky.

Taverna Fare

Only the best seasonal ingredients, usually just picked, caught or slaughtered, are found in the kitchen. A local farmer regularly stops by with a truckload of fresh vegetables and fruits or perhaps a lamb or pig to sell. A fisherman appears with his daily catch, and the cook pulls fresh greens from the backyard or a neighboring field. This local harvest, along with fragrant green olive oil, bouquets of aromatic herbs and a pantryful of spices, will be transformed into a handful of unpretentious yet irresistible braises, stews, grills and sautés.

Often a small blackboard lists what is offered; other times the waiter simply recites the options. Fresh seafood is usually showcased on the menu, and many establishments prompt their guests to make their own choices from a display of the fresh fish and shellfish on hand. A table laden with an assortment of appetizers—a *meze* selection in Greece and Turkey, *tapas* in Spain and *acepipes* in Portugal—is proudly offered, and diners are encouraged to pick out an array of different varieties to begin the feast.

A hearty soup or stew or grilled meat or fish is the classic centerpiece of the meal, accompanied with a simple pilaf or roasted potatoes and perhaps a salad or some cooked greens drizzled with olive oil. Desserts are most often a piece of fruit or cheese, or sometimes a creamy baked custard.

The Taverna Environment

Taverna-style establishments nearly always provide a rustic setting of rough stone or plank floors and plain wooden tables. Decorative hand-painted tiles or frescoes by a local artist might cover the walls, and wine casks are customarily stacked behind a long bar. There is no fancy china and only rarely are there table linens. The flatware is inexpensive, the pottery is sturdy and the glasses are

more often tumblers than stemware. Wine is offered in a carafe set on the table, which diners pour for themselves. The food is frequently served family style, on platters or in metal pans or terra-cotta casseroles straight from the oven, and second helpings are for the taking. Other times, in what might be a more gentrified establishment, each course arrives on individual plates. In either case, however, informality reigns.

INTRODUCTION

BEVERAGES

The Greek taverna and its Turkish, Portuguese and Spanish cousins traditionally act as showcases for locally produced wines and spirits. Thus, only rarely will you be shown a wine list at one of these establishments. Instead, the waiter will more likely plunk down a carafe of the most recent native vintage or, sensing your interest, may seek out an older bottle from a tiny wine cellar.

At the Greek Taverna

In Greece, the bite-sized snacks known as *meze* are often accompanied with beer, wine or the strong, anise-flavored spirit known as ouzo. A jigger or so of the clear liquid is poured into a tall glass to which water is customarily added, turning the mixture a cloudy white. Although ouzo may at first appear an odd partner to the savory taverna dishes, the faint licorice flavor is surprisingly complementary to the food, harmonizing in particular with the many vinaigrette-dressed *meze* offerings.

Resinated wines, their harsh bouquet reminiscent of turpentine, originated with the ancient Greek custom of storing grape wines in amphorae treated with tar, which infused the beverages with a unique piney taste. White retsina, served well chilled, is by the far the most popular of these frequently cask-stored wines. Try it paired with seafood and poultry.

The Greeks also bottle a large body of nonresinated wines, including the famed white Santorini and a few distinguished reds. During his Greek sojourn, Lord Byron enjoyed the smooth, sweet Muscat of the island of Samos, a fine companion to dessert. A glass of Metaxa brandy is also a favorite way to close a taverna meal.

At the Turkish Lokanta

Although nearly all Turks are Muslims and thus follow a religious teaching that forbids the drinking of alcoholic beverages, anise-scented *raki,* similar to Greek ouzo, is commonly drunk at a *lokanta*. Like ouzo, it is diluted with water to produce a kind of licorice cooler that is well suited to pairing with a *meze* selection. Well-chilled nonalcoholic drinks flavored with pomegranate or an almond and yogurt drink called *ayran* might also be served alongside taverna-style dishes.

At the Portuguese Tasca

Portugal produces hundreds of wines, most of them the product of small wineries and *cooperativas,* a fact that makes it difficult to find these agreeable bottlings beyond its borders. Since many of these local wines are often delivered to *tascas* in large barrels, they are customarily brought to the table in ceramic or earthenware pitchers. Of the many wines that might be served in this casual manner, *vinho verde,* one of the light, refreshing "prickly" wines, is especially popular. These young vintages are always served well chilled, and make wonderful aperitifs or accompaniments to fish and shellfish. There is also a wealth of hardy Portuguese reds. They are a good complement to robust meat and game stews.

Port and Madeira, the country's two great fortified wines, are the primary source of its importance in the wine world. White and tawny ports are usually served chilled as an aperitif, while the rubies are excellent poured after dinner to accompany cheeses, nuts and dried fruits.

Madeira wines range from the light and dry to sweet. Dry Madeiras are normally chilled and served as aperitifs, while sweet varieties complement fruits and desserts.

At the Spanish Taberna

In Spain, sherry is both the classic aperitif and accompaniment to *tapas.* The light, dry sherries are served chilled, at room temperature or over ice, while the stouter varieties as well as the sweet cream sherries are usually served at room temperature as a complement to dessert.

Although sangria is a popular fruit-filled wine punch, it is best offered as a refreshing beverage on a hot summer day rather than as an accompaniment to a meal. Instead, look to the considerable production of excellent Spanish wines for serving with classic *taberna* fare. The whites are well matched to the vast array of seafood dishes. The reds complement the heartier meat dishes.

Coffees

Around the Mediterranean, coffee is served both to cap off a meal and to revive the senses in the midafternoon. In Turkey and Greece, small cups of sweetened, thick, dark coffee are served with glasses of ice water as chasers for cutting the intensity of the brew. In Portugal, coffee generally takes the form of a *bica,* a short, strong demitasse brewed from richly aromatic beans, while the Spanish consume their *cafe* plain or with a splash of brandy or liqueur for a nice finish to an evening meal.

FRIED ALMONDS

Throughout Portugal, Spain and other Mediterranean countries, you'll find this addictive taverna snack served with drinks.

Vegetable oil or olive oil
Whole blanched almonds
Salt
Ground cayenne pepper, optional

In a deep frying pan, pour in oil to a depth of 2 inches (5 cm). Place over medium heat and heat to 350°F (180°C) on a deep-frying thermometer (or until an almond dropped into the oil sizzles immediately). Drop in a handful of the almonds and fry until golden, about 3 minutes. Using a slotted spoon, transfer to paper towels to drain. Repeat with the remaining almonds. Season to taste with salt and with cayenne, if using, and serve warm.

INTRODUCTION

BASIC RECIPES

In tavernas and similarly rustic establishments, most dishes are composed of little else than a few simple ingredients that have been either grilled, roasted or stewed. Such dishes might seem quite plain were it not for the redolent sauces with which they are customarily served. These sauces, some of which follow here, can transform anything from a small plate of roasted vegetables to a single skewer of grilled shrimp into a superb creation all its own.

GARLIC-POTATO SAUCE

SKORDALIA

Skordalia takes its name from skordo, *or "garlic." Different versions of the sauce are thickened with potato or with bread and nuts or with all three. Some recipes call for only vinegar, while others, such as this one, also add lemon juice. Serve as an accompaniment to fried fresh fish or salt cod, cooked beets, fried zucchini (courgette) or eggplant (aubergine), and greens.*

¾ cup (4 oz/125 g) blanched almonds or walnuts, optional

1 lb (500 g) baking potatoes or new potatoes, peeled and cut into 2-inch (5-cm) pieces

8 cloves garlic
  Coarse salt

3 tablespoons red wine vinegar, or to taste

¼ cup (2 fl oz/60 ml) fresh lemon juice

¾ cup (6 fl oz/180 ml) virgin olive oil
  Salt and freshly ground pepper

※ If using the nuts, preheat an oven to 350°F (180°C). Spread the almonds or walnuts on a baking sheet and place in the oven until toasted and fragrant, 8–10 minutes. Remove from the oven, let cool and chop. Set aside.

※ Meanwhile, bring a saucepan three-fourths full of water to a boil over high heat. Add the potato pieces and boil until tender when pierced with a fork, about 15 minutes. Drain well, return the potatoes to the pan and place over high heat for 1–2 minutes to evaporate the moisture, turning them to prevent scorching. Remove from the heat and, using a potato masher, mash the potatoes until smooth. Set aside.

※ In a mortar, combine the garlic with a little coarse salt and mash with a pestle until puréed. You should have about 2 tablespoons puréed garlic.

※ Stir the garlic into the potatoes and, using a whisk or fork, beat in 1 tablespoon of the vinegar, half of the lemon juice and half of the olive oil. Transfer to a food processor fitted with the metal blade. With the motor running, gradually add the remaining 2 tablespoons vinegar, the remaining lemon juice and olive oil, and the nuts, if using. Season to taste with more vinegar, if needed, and the salt and pepper. Transfer to a bowl and serve, or cover and refrigerate overnight. Bring to room temperature before serving.

Makes about 2¼ cups (18 fl oz/560 ml)

YOGURT-CUCUMBER SAUCE

TZATZIKI

Made from thick, rich sheep's milk yogurt, this tangy sauce is part of the meze *table in every Greek taverna. It can also be found in Turkey, where it is called* cacık. *For a similar consistency with cow's milk yogurt, you must first drain it of excess water. The sauce is delicious served with fried eggplant (aubergine) and zucchini (courgette), lamb chops or meatballs, or as a dip for pita bread.*

4 cups (32 oz/1 kg) plain yogurt
1 English (hothouse) cucumber, seeded and coarsely grated, or 2 small regular cucumbers, peeled, seeded and coarsely grated
   Salt
3 large cloves garlic, finely minced
1 tablespoon red wine vinegar or fresh lemon juice, or to taste
3 tablespoons olive oil
¼ cup (⅓ oz/10 g) chopped fresh mint or equal amounts chopped fresh mint and flat-leaf (Italian) parsley
   Freshly ground pepper

❊ Line a large sieve with cheesecloth (muslin), place it over a bowl and spoon the yogurt into the sieve.

Refrigerate for 4–6 hours to drain the excess water from the yogurt. You should have 1½–2 cups (12–16 oz/375–500 g) drained yogurt. Refrigerate until needed.

❊ Place the grated cucumber in a sieve or colander, salt it lightly and toss to mix. Let stand for 30 minutes to draw out the excess moisture.

❊ In a bowl, combine the drained yogurt, garlic, vinegar or lemon juice and olive oil and stir to mix well. Using a kitchen towel, squeeze the drained cucumber dry. Fold the cucumber into the yogurt mixture and then stir in the mint or mint and parsley. Season to taste with salt and pepper. Serve immediately, or cover and refrigerate overnight. Bring to room temperature before serving.

Makes about 2½ cups (20 fl oz/625 ml)

TOMATO-NUT SAUCE
SALSA ROMESCO

This Catalan sauce takes its name from a variety of mild dried pepper. For more spice, add some minced fresh jalapeño or more cayenne. In Catalonia, romesco is served with grilled shellfish and green onions. It is also wonderful on grilled fish, lamb, pork or leeks and asparagus or beets, and is addictive as a dipping sauce for fried potatoes.

2   dried ancho chili peppers

1   large red bell pepper (capsicum)

½   cup (2½ oz/75 g) blanched almonds

½   cup (2½ oz/75 g) hazelnuts (filberts)

2   tablespoons plus ⅔ cup (5 fl oz/ 160 ml) virgin olive oil

1   slice coarse-textured peasant bread, ½ inch (12 mm) thick, crust removed

3   large cloves garlic, minced

1   cup (6 oz/185 g) peeled, seeded, diced and well-drained tomatoes (fresh or canned)

1   tablespoon paprika

½   teaspoon ground cayenne pepper, or to taste

3   tablespoons red wine vinegar, or to taste

   Salt and freshly ground black pepper

※ Place the ancho chilies in a bowl, add hot water to cover and let stand for 1 hour.

※ Meanwhile, preheat a broiler (griller). Cut the bell pepper in half lengthwise and remove the stem, seeds and ribs. Place the pepper halves, cut sides down, on a baking sheet. Broil (grill) until the skins are blackened and blistered. Transfer the pepper halves to a plastic container, cover and let stand for 20 minutes. Peel off the skins, then chop the pepper. Set aside.

※ Preheat an oven to 350°F (180°C). Spread the almonds and hazelnuts on a baking sheet, keeping them separate. Toast in the oven until fragrant and the skins of the hazelnuts begin to loosen, 8–10 minutes. Spread the hazelnuts on a kitchen towel. Cover with a second towel and rub the towels against the nuts to remove the skins. Set the almonds and hazelnuts aside.

※ Drain the ancho chilies and remove the stems, seeds and ribs. Chop the chilies and set aside.

※ In a small sauté pan over medium heat, warm the 2 tablespoons olive oil. Add the bread and fry, turning once, until golden on both sides, about 5 minutes. Transfer the bread to a food processor fitted with the metal blade or to a blender. Add the ancho chilies, almonds and hazelnuts, bell pepper, garlic, tomatoes, paprika, the ½ teaspoon cayenne and the 3 tablespoons vinegar. Purée until smooth. With the motor running, gradually add the ⅔ cup (5 fl oz/160 ml) olive oil. The mixture should be the consistency of sour cream. Season to taste with salt and pepper. Let stand for 15 minutes to blend the flavors, then taste and adjust the seasoning with cayenne pepper or vinegar, if needed. Transfer to a bowl and serve, or cover and refrigerate for up to 1 month. Bring to room temperature before serving.

Makes about 2½ cups (20 fl oz/625 ml)

CHILI PEPPER SAUCE
MOLHO DE PIRI-PIRI

Piri-piri *is the Portuguese name
for an extremely hot variety of pepper
that traveled to Portugal via Angola.
Much of the pepper's heat comes from
the seeds, so use all or part of them,
depending upon how hot you want your
sauce. Serve this fiery condiment as a
marinade or sauce for grilled marinated
shrimp (prawns), lobster or chicken.*

½ cup (2 oz/60 g) coarsely chopped
  fresh hot red chili peppers
3 cloves garlic, finely minced
1 teaspoon kosher salt
1 cup (8 fl oz/250 ml) olive oil
¼ cup (2 fl oz/60 ml) red wine
  vinegar, optional

❋ Combine all of the ingredients in a
jar. Cover and let stand in a cool, dark
place for at least 1 week or for up to
1 month. Shake well before using.

Makes about 1½ cups (12 fl oz/375 ml)

MARINATED OLIVES
AZEITONAS

*Whichever of these two different prepara-
tions you choose, be sure to marinate the
olives for at least 2 days before setting
them out with drinks as part of a meze
or tapas table. They will keep very well
for up to a week in the refrigerator.*

FOR BLACK OLIVES
1 lb (500 g) brine-cured black
  olives, rinsed of brine
3 cloves garlic, crushed
1 teaspoon ground cumin
1 teaspoon red pepper flakes
  Olive oil

FOR GREEN OLIVES
1 lb (500 g) brine-cured green
  olives, rinsed of brine
4 cloves garlic, crushed
2 tablespoons dried oregano
2 thin orange or lemon zest strips
  Olive oil

❋ Select either the black or green
olives to prepare, or prepare both.
Combine all the ingredients in a bowl,
adding olive oil as needed to cover.
Toss well to combine. Cover and
refrigerate for at least 2 days. Bring
to room temperature before serving.

Makes 1 or 2 lb (500 g or 1 kg)

Appetizers

Whether you enter a Greek taverna, Turkish *lokanta,* Spanish *taberna,* or Portuguese *tasca,* your first sight will likely be of a table spread with an irresistible display of room-temperature dishes. In Greece and Turkey, these delectable appetizer offerings are known as *mezethes,* in Spain they are *tapas* and in Portugal *acepipes.* They will be brought to you one or two at a time, usually each on its own plate. A waiter will circulate through the room with the hot items, offering perhaps just a single fabulous taste with each visit to your table. Don't be shy, for among these dishes will be much-requested specialties that cannot be found elsewhere.

In fact, you may want to make a whole meal of these tempting plates, just as the locals often do. A few tastes will convince you: Dip your bread into a mound of cool roasted eggplant or serve it alongside a platter of sizzling garlic shrimp. Try a piping hot fritter of salt cod or zucchini, or lace a skewer of just-fried mussels with the nut-thickened sauce known as *tarator.*

These widely varied plates will introduce you to the wealth of savory flavors to follow in the rest of the taverna meal. Indeed, there is no better way to know the palate—the signature tastes of a country—than through these tantalizing appetizers.

Garlic Shrimp

In Spanish tabernas, *these shrimp—fragrant with garlic and olive oil—*
are brought to the table sizzling in a little metal pan. Have plenty of bread on hand
to sop up the delicious pan juices. Serve with lemon wedges, if desired.

¼ cup (2 fl oz/60 ml) olive oil
4 large cloves garlic, finely minced
1 teaspoon red pepper flakes
1 lb (500 g) medium shrimp (prawns), peeled and deveined
2 tablespoons fresh lemon juice
2 tablespoons dry sherry
1 teaspoon paprika
Salt and freshly ground black pepper
Chopped fresh flat-leaf (Italian) parsley for garnish

In a sauté pan over medium heat, warm the olive oil. Add the garlic and red pepper flakes and sauté for 1 minute. Raise the heat to high and add the shrimp, lemon juice, sherry and paprika. Stir well, then sauté, stirring briskly, until the shrimp turn pink and curl slightly, about 3 minutes. Season to taste with salt and pepper and sprinkle with parsley. Serve hot.

Serves 4

Zucchini Fritters

Although these fritters are at their best when hot, in many Turkish cafés they are served at room temperature accompanied by the yogurt-cucumber sauce called cacık *(recipe on page 13). Traditionally part of the* meze *course, they also make a nice side dish for seafood, poultry or lamb.*

1   lb (500 g) small zucchini (cour-
    gettes), coarsely grated
    Salt
½   lb (250 g) feta cheese, or equal
    parts feta and kasseri or ricotta
6   green (spring) onions, minced
½   cup (½ oz/15 g) chopped fresh
    dill
¼   cup (⅓ oz/10 g) chopped fresh
    mint
¼   cup (⅓ oz/10 g) chopped fresh
    flat-leaf (Italian) parsley
3   eggs, lightly beaten
1   cup (5 oz/155 g) all-purpose
    (plain) flour
    Freshly ground pepper
    Peanut oil for frying

※ Place the zucchini in a sieve or colander, salt it lightly and toss to mix. Let stand for 30 minutes to draw out the excess moisture. Using a kitchen towel, squeeze the zucchini dry and place it in a bowl. Crumble the cheese over the zucchini and add the green onions, dill, mint, parsley, eggs, flour and salt and pepper to taste. Stir to mix well.

※ In a deep frying pan over medium-high heat, pour in the peanut oil to a depth of ¼ inch (6 mm). When the oil is hot, using a serving spoon, drop spoonfuls of the batter into the oil, being careful not to crowd the pan. Fry, turning once, until nicely browned on both sides, 2–3 minutes per side. Using a slotted spoon or spatula, transfer the fritters to paper towels to drain. Keep warm until all the fritters are cooked.

※ Arrange the fritters on a warmed platter and serve hot.

Serves 8 as an appetizer, 4 as a side dish

Potato Omelet

Unlike most omelets, this classic Spanish tapa *is usually served at room temperature and, as the name* tortilla *suggests, it has a flat, cakelike shape. A large nonstick frying pan is ideal for cooking the omelet, which also makes a good main course for four at lunchtime.*

½ cup (4 fl oz/125 ml) plus
   3 tablespoons olive oil
2 lb (1 kg) baking potatoes,
   peeled and sliced ¼ inch
   (6 mm) thick
   Salt and freshly ground pepper
2 onions, thinly sliced
6 eggs, lightly beaten
   Chopped fresh flat-leaf (Italian)
   parsley for garnish

❋ In a large frying pan over medium heat, warm the ½ cup (4 fl oz/125 ml) olive oil. Add half of the potatoes and fry, turning as needed, until tender but not browned, 10–12 minutes. (Don't worry if the slices stick to one another a little.) Using a slotted spatula, transfer to a platter and season to taste with salt and pepper. Repeat with the remaining potatoes. Set the potatoes and the frying pan aside.

❋ In a small sauté pan over medium heat, warm 2 tablespoons of the olive oil. Add the onions and sauté until soft and golden, 15–20 minutes. Transfer the onions to a large bowl and let cool slightly. Stir in the eggs and season to taste with salt and pepper. Fold in the fried potatoes.

❋ Place the large frying pan over low heat and warm the oil that remains in it. When the oil is hot, pour in the potato-egg mixture and cook until the top of the omelet is set and the bottom is golden, 8–10 minutes. Invert a large plate on top of the frying pan and invert the plate and pan together, unmolding the omelet browned side up. Add the remaining 1 tablespoon olive oil to the pan and slide the omelet back into the pan, browned side up. Continue to cook until golden brown on the second side, about 4 minutes longer.

❋ Turn the omelet out onto a serving plate, sprinkle with parsley and cut into wedges. Serve hot or at room temperature.

Serves 6–8

Salt Cod Fritters

These crispy fritters are among the most popular acepipes in Portugal. Made from the preserved fish that has long been a staple of the Iberian peninsula and other Mediterranean countries, they are also a regular feature on the menus of Spanish tapas bars.

½ lb (250 g) salt cod

2 boiling potatoes, about 10 oz (315 g) total weight, unpeeled
  Milk, if needed

2 tablespoons olive oil, plus olive oil or vegetable oil for deep-frying

1 small onion, minced

2 cloves garlic, finely minced

2 eggs

3 tablespoons chopped fresh flat-leaf (Italian) parsley

3 tablespoons chopped fresh cilantro (fresh coriander)
  Pinch of ground cayenne pepper
  Freshly ground black pepper

※ Place the salt cod in a bowl and add cold water to cover. Cover and refrigerate for 36–48 hours, changing the water 4 or 5 times. Drain the cod well, rinse in cold water and place in a saucepan. Add water to cover and slowly bring to a low boil. Reduce the heat to low and simmer gently until the cod is tender when pierced with a fork and flakes easily, 15–20 minutes.

※ Meanwhile, place the potatoes in a saucepan with water to cover and bring to a boil over high heat. Boil until tender when pierced with a fork, 10–15 minutes. Drain well and when cool enough to handle, peel, place in a bowl and mash with a potato masher or a fork. Set aside.

※ When the cod is done, drain and let cool. Using your fingers, break up the cod, removing any errant bones, skin or tough parts. Taste it. If it seems too salty, heat enough milk to cover the cod. Place the cod in a bowl, add the hot milk to cover and let stand for 30 minutes, then drain.

※ Place the cod in a food processor fitted with the metal blade and, using on-off pulses, process until coarsely chopped. Transfer to a bowl.

※ In a small sauté pan over medium heat, warm the 2 tablespoons olive oil. Add the onion and sauté until tender, about 8 minutes. Add the garlic and sauté for 2 minutes longer. Remove from the heat.

※ Add the potatoes and onion to the cod and mix well. Beat in the eggs, parsley and cilantro. Season to taste with cayenne and black pepper. (The mixture should be just stiff enough to hold a shape. If it is too stiff, beat in a little milk.) Using a spoon, form into balls about 1 inch (2.5 cm) in diameter.

※ In a deep, heavy frying pan, pour in oil to a depth of 3 inches (7.5 cm) and heat to 375°F (190°C) on a deep-frying thermometer (or until a little bit of the fritter mixture dropped into the oil sizzles immediately). Slip the balls into the oil, a few at a time, and fry, turning occasionally, until golden, about 4 minutes. Using a slotted spoon, transfer to paper towels to drain. Keep warm until all the fritters are cooked.

※ Arrange the fritters on a warmed platter and serve hot.

Serves 6–8

Stuffed Grape Leaves

No Greek meze *table is complete without dolmas, the family of stuffed vine or cabbage leaves and vegetables such as tomatoes, eggplants (aubergines) and zucchini (courgettes). These popular rice-filled grape leaves, known as* dolmades, *are usually served at room temperature with lemon wedges or yogurt. One 8-ounce (250-g) jar of grape leaves should provide enough for filling and lining the pan.*

1 cup (7 oz/220 g) long-grain white rice, preferably basmati

¼ cup (1½ oz/45 g) currants

¼ cup (1 oz/30 g) pine nuts, optional

¾ cup (6 fl oz/180 ml) olive oil

2 cups (10 oz/315 g) finely chopped yellow onion

1 teaspoon salt, plus salt to taste

1 cup (3 oz/90 g) finely chopped green (spring) onions

1 teaspoon ground allspice

1 teaspoon ground cinnamon

½ cup (3 oz/90 g) peeled, seeded, chopped and drained tomatoes (fresh or canned), optional

½ cup (¾ oz/20 g) chopped fresh flat-leaf (Italian) parsley

¼ cup (⅓ oz/10 g) chopped fresh mint or dill

¾ cup (6 fl oz/180 ml) hot water
Freshly ground pepper

36 grape leaves preserved in brine, plus grape leaves for lining pan, optional

2 cups (16 fl oz/500 ml) boiling water
Fresh lemon juice, plus lemon wedges for serving

※ Place the rice in a bowl, add cold water to cover and let stand for 30 minutes. At the same time, place the currants in a small bowl, add hot water to cover and let stand for 30 minutes until plumped. Drain the rice and currants and set aside.

※ Meanwhile, if using the pine nuts, preheat an oven to 350°F (180°C). Spread the nuts in a small pan and place in the oven until toasted and fragrant, 6–8 minutes. Set aside.

※ In a large sauté pan over medium heat, warm ½ cup (4 fl oz/120 ml) of the olive oil. Add the yellow onion and the 1 teaspoon salt and sauté until softened, about 5 minutes. Add the green onions and sauté until softened, about 5 minutes longer. Add the allspice, cinnamon and drained rice and cook, stirring, until the rice is opaque, about 4 minutes. Add the chopped tomatoes (if using), parsley, mint or dill, currants and hot water and cook, uncovered, until the water is absorbed and the rice is about half cooked, about 10 minutes. Stir in the pine nuts, if using. Season to taste with salt and pepper. Let cool.

※ Rinse the grape leaves in cool water and cut off the stems. Working in batches, lay them out on a table,

shiny side down. Place a tablespoonful of the rice filling near the stem end of each leaf, fold the bottom end over the filling, then fold in the sides and roll up. Do not roll too tightly, as the rice will expand during cooking. Set aside, seam side down.

※ When all of the filling has been used, select a baking pan or large, deep frying pan that will hold the stuffed grape leaves in a single layer and line with more grape leaves, if using. Arrange the stuffed grape leaves in the pan, seam sides down. Place a heavy plate on top to keep the leaves from unrolling while cooking, then pour the boiling water and the remaining ¼ cup (2 fl oz/ 60 ml) olive oil around the leaves.

※ Cover and simmer gently over very low heat until the rice and leaves are tender, about 45 minutes. Remove from the heat and remove the plate. Sprinkle with a little lemon juice, let cool, then serve with lemon wedges. Or cover and refrigerate for up to 2 days; bring to room temperature before serving.

Makes 36 pieces

Fried Cheese

This taverna standby is named for the two-handled pan in which it is fried. Some cooks include the flourish of flambéing the cheese with brandy, but this dramatic touch adds little flavor and may toughen the cheese. Offer freshly cracked pepper and some crusty bread at the table, and pour a good ouzo.

½ lb (250 g) kefalotiri or kasseri cheese
About ¼ cup (1½ oz/45 g) all-purpose (plain) flour
1 teaspoon freshly ground pepper
Olive oil for frying
1 tablespoon dried oregano
2 tablespoons fresh lemon juice, plus lemon wedges for serving

❊ Cut the cheese into slices ½ inch (12 mm) thick, about 3 inches (7.5 cm) long and 2 inches (5 cm) wide. Rinse the cheese in cold water to remove excess salt, then pat dry with paper towels. Spread the flour on a plate and season it with the pepper. Dip the cheese pieces in the seasoned flour, turning to coat evenly on both sides.

❊ In a large, heavy sauté pan, pour in olive oil to a depth of ¼ inch (6 mm). Place over high heat until very hot but not smoking. Working with 2 or 3 cheese pieces at a time, carefully slip the pieces into the hot oil and fry, turning once, until golden brown on both sides, about 2 minutes per side. Using a slotted spoon, transfer the cheese to paper towels to drain. Keep warm until all the pieces are cooked.

❊ Arrange the cheese on a warmed platter and sprinkle with the oregano and lemon juice. Serve hot with lemon wedges on the side.

Serves 4

Fried Mussels with Nut Sauce

These crispy mussels are a popular menu item at the street stands that line busy wharves and open-air markets throughout Turkey. The accompanying nut sauce, known as tarator, *can be thickened with hazelnuts (filberts) or almonds in place of the walnuts; it is also good served with cooked vegetables and fish.*

NUT SAUCE

1	cup (4 oz/125 g) walnuts
1	tablespoon finely minced garlic
1½	cups (3 oz/90 g) fresh bread crumbs
⅓	cup (3 fl oz/80 ml) olive oil
3	tablespoons red or white wine vinegar or fresh lemon juice, or to taste
	Salt and freshly ground pepper
40	large mussels in the shell
1	cup (8 fl oz/250 ml) water
1½	cups (7½ oz/235 g) all-purpose (plain) flour
	Peanut oil for deep-frying

※ Soak 10 small wooden skewers in water to cover for at least 30 minutes.

※ To make the nut sauce, preheat an oven to 350°F (180°C). Spread the walnuts on a baking sheet and place in the oven until toasted and fragrant, 8–10 minutes. Let cool, then place in a food processor fitted with the metal blade or in a blender. Add the garlic and bread crumbs and use rapid on-off pulses to combine. Add the olive oil and vinegar or lemon juice and purée until smooth; thin to a spoonable consistency with water, if necessary. Season to taste with salt, pepper and more vinegar or lemon juice, if needed; transfer to a bowl. Set aside.

※ Discard any mussels that do not close to the touch, then scrub the mussels well under running water.

※ Pour water to a depth of 1 inch (2.5 cm) in a large, wide sauté pan and add the mussels. Place over high heat, cover and cook until the mussels open, 3–4 minutes. Drain the mussels and discard any that have not opened. Remove the mussels from their shells, gently pulling off their beards. Drain the skewers and thread 4 mussels on each skewer.

※ In a wide, shallow bowl, combine the water and flour and stir to make a thin batter. Set aside.

※ In a deep frying pan or wok, pour in peanut oil to a depth of 2–3 inches (5–7.5 cm). Heat to 375°F (190°C) on a deep-frying thermometer (or until a tiny bit of the batter dropped into the oil sizzles immediately).

※ Working in batches, dip the mussel-loaded skewers into the batter, then slip them into the oil. Fry, turning as needed, until golden on all sides, 2–3 minutes. Using tongs, transfer to paper towels to drain. Keep warm until all the mussels are cooked.

※ To serve, arrange the skewers on a serving dish. Serve hot with the sauce on the side.

Serves 4–8

Grilled Eggplant Salad

Although technically termed a salad, this purée is often served as a spread alongside tomato wedges, olives and bread. If you prefer a smoky flavor, grill or broil the eggplants; for a milder taste, roast them in a 400°F (200°C) oven, or cook them on a stove-top griddle.

3 cups (24 oz/750 g) plain yogurt
3 large globe eggplants (aubergines), 2½–3 lb (1.25–1.5 kg) total weight
3 tablespoons fresh lemon juice
3 cloves garlic
1 teaspoon salt, plus salt to taste
⅓ cup (3 fl oz/80 ml) olive oil
⅔ cup (2½ oz/75 g) finely chopped walnuts, optional
1 or 2 pinches ground cayenne pepper or minced fresh jalapeño chili pepper, optional
Freshly ground black pepper
Chopped fresh flat-leaf (Italian) parsley for garnish

❈ Line a large sieve with cheesecloth (muslin), place it over a bowl and spoon the yogurt into the sieve. Refrigerate for 4–6 hours to drain off the excess water. You should have 1–1½ cups (8–12 oz/250–375 g) drained yogurt.

❈ Preheat a broiler (griller) or prepare a fire in a charcoal grill. Using a fork, pierce the skin on either side of each eggplant. Place on a broiler pan or a grill rack and broil or grill, turning as needed, until blistered, charred and soft throughout when pierced with a knife, about 20 minutes. (If the eggplants are darkening quickly and are not softening, finish cooking them in an oven preheated to 400°F/200°C.) Set aside to cool.

❈ When the eggplants are cool enough to handle, cut them in half and scoop out the pulp, discarding as many seeds as possible.

❈ For a smooth purée, place the pulp in a food processor fitted with the metal blade and purée until free of lumps. For a chunkier purée, chop with a knife on a cutting board. Transfer the purée to a serving bowl. Add the lemon juice and mix well.

❈ In a mortar, combine the garlic with the 1 teaspoon salt and mash with a pestle until puréed. Add the purée to the eggplant along with the olive oil and, if using, the walnuts and the cayenne or jalapeño. Mix well and season to taste with salt and pepper. Garnish with parsley and serve.

Serves 4–6

Lamb Pizza

*Open-faced meat pies like these are popular café food in Syria, Lebanon and Israel, as well
as in Turkey. The dough is a cross between that used for an Italian pizza and Turkish pide bread.
You can also shape it into smaller 4-inch (10-cm) pies. Add the chilies if you prefer a little heat.*

SPONGE
1	envelope (2½ teaspoons) active dry yeast
1	teaspoon sugar
½	cup (4 fl oz/125 ml) lukewarm water (105°F/43°C)
½	cup (2½ oz/75 g) unbleached bread flour

DOUGH
4½	cups (22½ oz/700 g) unbleached bread flour
2	teaspoons salt
2	tablespoons olive oil
1½	cups (12 fl oz/375 ml) lukewarm water (105°F/43°C)

LAMB FILLING
2	tablespoons olive oil
1	large onion, finely chopped
4	cloves garlic, minced
1	lb (500 g) ground (minced) lamb
1½	cups (9 oz/280 g) peeled, seeded and chopped tomatoes
½	cup (2 oz/60 g) minced mild green chili peppers, optional
½	teaspoon ground allspice
1	teaspoon ground cinnamon
½	cup (¾ oz/20 g) chopped fresh flat-leaf (Italian) parsley
	Salt and ground black pepper
¼	cup (1 oz/30 g) pine nuts
	Olive oil for brushing on pizzas
¼	cup (⅓ oz/10 g) chopped fresh mint

❊ To make the sponge, in a small bowl, dissolve the yeast and sugar in the lukewarm water. Stir in the flour and let stand in a warm place until bubbly, about 5 minutes.

❊ *To make the dough in an electric stand mixer,* place the flour in the bowl of a mixer and add the sponge, salt, olive oil and lukewarm water. Using the paddle attachment, mix on low speed to combine. Then attach the dough hook and beat on medium speed until the dough is smooth, elastic and pulls cleanly from the bowl sides, 5–6 minutes.

❊ *To make the dough by hand,* place the flour in a large bowl and add the sponge, salt, olive oil and lukewarm water. Stir until a soft dough forms, then turn out onto a lightly floured work surface and knead until smooth and elastic, about 10–12 minutes.

❊ Shape the dough into a ball, place in an oiled bowl and turn to coat evenly. Cover the bowl with plastic wrap and let rise in a warm place until doubled, 45–60 minutes.

❊ Meanwhile, make the lamb filling: In a large sauté pan over medium heat, warm the olive oil. Add the onion and sauté until tender, about 10 minutes. Add the garlic and lamb, raise the heat to high and sauté until it begins to brown, 5–8 minutes. Add the tomatoes, chilies (if using), allspice and cinnamon and cook uncovered, stirring occasionally, for about 30 minutes. The mixture should be very thick. Stir in half of the parsley and season to taste with salt and pepper. Let cool.

❊ Meanwhile, turn out the dough onto a lightly floured work surface and knead briefly. Divide into 12 equal portions and form each portion into a ball. Place the balls on the work surface, cover with a kitchen towel and let rest for 30 minutes.

❊ Preheat an oven to 350°F (180°C). Spread the pine nuts in a small pan and toast in the oven until fragrant, 6–8 minutes. Let cool.

❊ Raise the oven temperature to 500°F (260°C). Roll out each ball of dough into a round 6 inches (15 cm) in diameter. Place the rounds spaced well apart on baking sheets. Brush lightly with olive oil and then divide the filling evenly among them, leaving a ½-inch (12-mm) border uncovered. Sprinkle evenly with the pine nuts.

❊ Bake until the crust is golden, about 6 minutes. Sprinkle with the remaining parsley and the mint and serve hot.

Makes twelve 6-inch (15-cm) pizzas

Cheese–Filled Pastries

Although these popular cheese-filled pastries are commonly shaped as triangles for the popular borek, *they are equally delicious in the form of plump, round cigars. They can be filled and shaped up to 2 days in advance and refrigerated, covered, in a single layer on a parchment-lined baking sheet; fry just before serving.*

6 oz (185 g) feta cheese, crumbled

6 oz (185 g) cottage cheese or shredded Monterey Jack cheese

2 eggs, lightly beaten

¼ cup (⅓ oz/10 g) chopped fresh flat-leaf (Italian) parsley

2 tablespoons chopped fresh dill

¼ teaspoon freshly grated nutmeg
Salt and freshly ground pepper

9 sheets filo dough (about 6 oz/ 185 g), thawed in the refrigerator if frozen

¼ cup (2 oz/60 g) clarified unsalted butter, melted
Peanut or olive oil for deep-frying

※ In a bowl, combine the feta cheese, cottage cheese or jack cheese, eggs, parsley, dill and nutmeg. Mix well, then season to taste with salt and pepper.

※ Remove the filo sheets from their package and lay the stacked sheets flat on a work surface. Cut the stack into quarters, forming squares measuring about 6 inches (15 cm) on a side. Cover the stack with a damp towel or plastic wrap to prevent the sheets from drying out. Working with 1 square at a time, place it on the work surface, brush it lightly with butter and then spoon a narrow strip of the cheese mixture (2–3 tablespoons) along one end, leaving a ¾-inch (2-cm) border on the bottom and sides. Fold in the sides, bring the bottom up over the filling and then roll up like a cigar. Seal the edge with a little water and repeat with the remaining squares and filling until all have been used.

※ In a deep frying pan, pour in peanut or olive oil to a depth of 2½ inches (6 cm) and heat to 350°F (180°C) on a deep-frying thermometer (or until a tiny piece of filo dropped into the oil turns golden within moments). Working in batches, carefully slip the rolls into the hot oil and fry, turning as needed, until golden on all sides, about 5 minutes. Do not crowd the pan. Using a slotted spoon or tongs, transfer to paper towels to drain.

※ Arrange the rolls on a warmed platter and serve hot.

Makes 36 rolls

Spinach Filo Pie

One of Greece's best-known dishes, this pie can also be served as a side dish or in larger portions as a main dish. Tablespoons of the same mixture can be used to fill tiropetes, little triangles folded from 3-inch (7.5-cm) strips cut lengthwise from filo sheets and brushed with clarified butter; they bake in 10–15 minutes.

1½ lb (750 g) spinach

3 tablespoons olive oil

½ cup (1½ oz/45 g) chopped green (spring) onions

½ cup (¾ oz/20 g) chopped fresh flat-leaf (Italian) parsley

½ cup (¾ oz/20 g) chopped fresh dill

¾ lb (375 g) feta cheese, crumbled

1 cup (8 oz/250 g) cottage cheese, if needed

3 eggs, lightly beaten

1 teaspoon freshly grated nutmeg
Salt and freshly ground pepper

18 sheets filo dough (¾ lb/375 g), thawed in the refrigerator if frozen

½ cup (4 oz/125 g) clarified unsalted butter, melted

Remove the stems from the spinach, chop the leaves coarsely and rinse well in several changes of water. Drain and set aside.

In a large frying pan over medium heat, warm the olive oil. Add the green onions and sauté until tender, about 5 minutes. Transfer to a bowl.

Add the spinach to the same pan and place over high heat. Cook, turning the spinach with tongs or a fork, until wilted, about 4 minutes. (The leaves will wilt in their own moisture.) Transfer to a sieve and drain well, pressing out the excess moisture with the back of a spoon.

Chop the spinach coarsely. Add it to the green onions, then stir in the parsley, dill and feta cheese. If the feta is salty, add the cottage cheese to mellow the overall flavor. Add the eggs and nutmeg and stir well. Season to taste with salt and pepper. Set aside.

Butter an 11-by-16-by-2½-inch (28-by-40-by-6-cm) baking dish. Remove the filo sheets from their package, lay them flat on a work surface and cover with a damp towel or plastic wrap to prevent them from drying out. Lay a filo sheet in the prepared dish and brush it lightly with the butter. Top with 8 more filo sheets, brushing each one with butter. Spread the spinach mixture evenly over the filo layers. Then top with the remaining 9 filo sheets, again brushing each sheet lightly with the butter, including the top sheet. Cover and refrigerate the pie for 30 minutes so the butter will set.

Meanwhile, preheat an oven to 350°F (180°C).

Using a sharp knife, cut the pie into 16 equal pieces. Bake until golden brown, about 30 minutes. Remove from the oven and let stand for 5 minutes. Recut the pieces and serve hot.

Makes 16 pieces

Soups and Vegetables

When you order soups in a Mediterranean taverna, rarely will they be refined light broths. More often they are hearty concoctions, given body by the addition of white beans or lentils, rice, pasta or stale bread, or they are studded with meatballs or pieces of chicken or fish. These robust bowls are meant to satisfy rather than titillate, and they can be a whole meal with just an appetizer to start and some good crusty bread alongside.

Fresh vegetables maintain an equally prominent place in the Mediterranean diet. In addition to their popularity in the region's soups and stews, they are equally at home served plain with just a drizzle of olive oil or in combination with any of an array of grains.

A delectable pilaf, enriched with eggplant and tomato, can serve as a main course. So, too, can stuffed tomatoes and sweet bell peppers, both glistening with olive oil and served right from the vessels in which they are baked. Side dishes of spinach or other cooked greens arrive on platters, with a garnish of lemon. Fried vegetables are delivered to the table at the last minute, sizzling hot and waiting to be dipped into a sprightly sauce. Even a simple Greek salad appears effortlessly delicious because, in every case, only the best seasonal vegetables have been used.

41

Chilled Tomato Soup

This peasant soup from Andalusia was originally made with crumbled bread, water, oil and vinegar. After the Spanish conquistadores returned from the New World with tomatoes and peppers, gazpacho evolved into the refreshing summer soup we know today.

2 slices day-old, coarse-textured peasant bread, crusts removed
1 small onion, chopped
2 cloves garlic, minced
1 small cucumber, peeled, seeded and coarsely chopped
2 lb (1 kg) fresh, ripe tomatoes, peeled, seeded and coarsely chopped
2 small green bell peppers (capsicums), seeded, deribbed and coarsely chopped
6 tablespoons (3 fl oz/90 ml) virgin olive oil
3 tablespoons red wine vinegar
Salt and freshly ground pepper
Ice water or part ice water and part chilled tomato juice, if needed

GARLIC CROUTONS
2 slices coarse-textured peasant bread
¼ cup (2 fl oz/60 ml) olive oil
1 teaspoon chopped garlic

✖ Place the bread slices in a bowl, add water to cover and let stand until soft, 3–5 minutes. Remove the bread and squeeze it dry with your hands.

✖ In a blender or a food processor fitted with the metal blade, combine the soaked bread, onion, garlic, cucumber, most of the tomatoes and 1 of the bell peppers. Process until smooth or chunky, as you like. Pour into a bowl.

✖ Finely chop the remaining tomatoes and the bell pepper and stir them into the bowl. Then stir in the olive oil and vinegar and season to taste with salt and pepper. If the soup is too thick, add a little ice water or a mixture of ice water and tomato juice. Cover and refrigerate until well chilled, or for up to 3 days.

✖ To make the garlic croutons, cut the bread slices into ½-inch (12-mm) cubes. In a large sauté pan over medium-high heat, warm the olive oil. Add the garlic and sauté, stirring, for 1 minute. Add the bread cubes and sauté until golden brown on all sides, 4–5 minutes. Using a slotted spoon, transfer the croutons to paper towels to drain.

✖ Ladle the soup into chilled bowls, top with the croutons and serve.

Serves 4

Bread Soup with Cilantro, Garlic and Poached Egg

This Portuguese soup from the province of Alentejo is known as a sopa seca, *or "dry soup," because its primary ingredient is bread. Each serving is topped with a poached egg that the diner must break with a spoon and swirl into the soup.*

1	tablespoon minced garlic
1	teaspoon salt
1	cup (1½ oz/40 g) chopped fresh cilantro (fresh coriander) Pinch of red pepper flakes, optional
½	cup (4 fl oz/120 ml) olive oil
3	thick slices coarse-textured peasant bread, crusts removed, cut into 1½-inch (4-cm) cubes (about 6 cups/12 oz/375 g)
4	eggs
3–4	cups (24–32 fl oz/750 ml–1 l) chicken stock, optional

❈ In a mortar, combine the garlic, salt, ½ cup (¾ oz/20 g) of the cilantro and the red pepper flakes, if using. Mash with a pestle to form a paste. Add ¼ cup (2 fl oz/60 ml) of the olive oil, 1 tablespoon at a time, and mix until well blended. Evenly divide the garlic paste among 4 warmed soup bowls and keep warm.

❈ Preheat an oven to 350°F (180°C). Brush the bread cubes with the remaining ¼ cup (2 fl oz/60 ml) olive oil and toast in the oven, turning a few times, until golden brown, 8–10 minutes.

❈ Distribute the bread cubes evenly among the soup bowls and toss them with the garlic mixture.

❈ In a deep frying pan, bring a generous amount of water to a rolling boil. Reduce the heat to medium-low so that the water barely simmers.

Crack each egg and gently release it just above the surface of the water. Simmer undisturbed until the whites are set but soft and the yolks are still runny, about 3 minutes. Using a slotted spoon, carefully remove the eggs and set aside on a plate.

❈ You may use the egg-poaching water (you will need 3–4 cups/24–32 fl oz/750 ml–1 l) for finishing the soup or you may use stock. Bring the water or stock to a boil and pour it over the bread cubes in each soup bowl, using only as much as needed to cover the bread. Carefully slip a poached egg into the center of each bowl. Sprinkle with the remaining ½ cup (¾ oz/20 g) cilantro. Serve hot.

Serves 4

"Green" Soup with Kale and Potatoes

*The dark green Galician cabbage used by Portuguese cooks for this winter soup
is not easily found outside of Portugal, but kale or collard greens can be substituted.
Bowls of the soup are often drizzled with chili pepper sauce (recipe on page 15).*

¼ cup (2 fl oz/60 ml) plus
   4 teaspoons olive oil

1 large yellow onion, chopped

2 cloves garlic, finely minced

3 baking potatoes, about 1 lb
   (500 g) total weight, peeled and
   sliced ¼ inch (6 mm) thick

6 cups (48 fl oz/1.5 l) water

2 teaspoons salt, plus salt to taste

¾ lb (375 g) kale or collard greens

¼ lb (125 g) *chouriço* or *linguiça*
   sausage
   Freshly ground pepper

※ In a large saucepan over medium heat, warm the ¼ cup (2 fl oz/60 ml) olive oil. Add the onion and sauté until tender, about 8 minutes. Add the garlic and potatoes and sauté over medium-high heat for a few minutes longer. Add the water and the 2 teaspoons salt. Cover and simmer over medium heat until the potatoes are very soft when pierced with a fork, about 20 minutes.

※ Meanwhile, rinse the greens well, drain and remove the tough stems. Working in batches, stack the leaves, roll them up like a cigar and cut crosswise into very thin strips. Set aside.

※ In a sauté pan over medium heat, cook the sausage, turning to brown all sides, until firm and cooked through, about 10 minutes. Let cool, then cut into slices ½ inch (12 mm) thick. Set aside.

※ When the potatoes are ready, remove from the heat and, using a wooden spoon or a potato masher, mash them to a purée in the water in the pan. Return the pan to low heat, add the sliced sausage and cook, stirring, for 5 minutes. Add the greens, stir well and simmer, uncovered, for 3–5 minutes. (Do not overcook; the greens should remain bright green and slightly crunchy.) Season to taste with salt and pepper.

※ Ladle the soup into warmed bowls, drizzle each serving with 1 teaspoon olive oil and serve hot.

Serves 4

Fish Soup

This soup takes its name from the kettle—kakavi—in which it is cooked. You can be as lavish as you like and use clams and scallops in place of the mussels and shrimp. Kakavia can be a rich first course or a meal in itself. Thick slices of grilled bread make a delicious accompaniment.

2   lb (1 kg) mussels

4   lb (2 kg) assorted thick fish fillets such as bass, flounder, halibut, haddock, snapper, cod and grouper
   Salt

½   cup (4 fl oz/125 ml) olive oil

2   cups (7 oz/220 g) sliced yellow onions

1   cup (3 oz/90 g) sliced leeks, carefully washed

4   cloves garlic, finely minced

2   celery stalks, chopped

1½   cups (9 oz/280 g) peeled, seeded and chopped tomatoes (fresh or canned)

4   fresh thyme sprigs

1   bay leaf

½   cup (½ oz/20 g) chopped fresh flat-leaf (Italian) parsley

1   cup (8 fl oz/250 ml) dry white wine

7   cups (56 fl oz/1.75 ml) water

1   lb (500 g) shrimp (prawns), peeled and deveined
   Fresh lemon juice
   Freshly ground pepper

❊ Discard any mussels that do not close to the touch, then scrub the mussels under running water and remove their beards. Place in a bowl and refrigerate until needed.

❊ Cut the fish fillets into 1½-inch (4-cm) pieces. Place on a plate, sprinkle with salt and refrigerate until needed.

❊ In a large saucepan or kettle over medium heat, warm the olive oil. Add the onions and leeks and sauté until translucent, about 8 minutes. Add the garlic, celery, tomatoes, thyme, bay leaf and ¼ cup (¼ oz/ 10 g) of the parsley and sauté for about 2 minutes longer.

❊ Add the wine and water and bring to a boil over high heat. Reduce the heat to medium and simmer for 15 minutes. Add the fish pieces, cover and cook for 5 minutes. Add the shrimp and mussels, re-cover and cook until the mussels open, 3–4 minutes. Discard any mussels that have not opened.

❊ Season to taste with lemon juice, salt and pepper. Ladle into warmed bowls. Sprinkle with the remaining ¼ cup (¼ oz/10 g) parsley. Serve hot.

Serves 12 as a first course, 6 as a main course

Meatball Soup with Egg and Lemon

*Avgolemono is the Greek term for the classic Mediterranean egg-and-lemon mixture
used as a thickener for soups or stews. In Turkey, the same blend is called terbiyeli. While simple
versions of this soup include just rice, and others call for chicken and rice, leeks and celery and
even fish, the most interesting and filling interpretations feature these little meatballs.*

1 lb (500 g) ground (minced) lean beef or lamb

1 cup (5 oz/155 g) grated or finely minced onion

6 tablespoons (2½ oz/75 g) long-grain white rice or ½ cup (2 oz/60 g) fine dried bread crumbs

½ cup (½ oz/20 g) chopped fresh flat-leaf (Italian) parsley

2 tablespoons chopped fresh mint or dill

3 eggs
Salt and freshly ground pepper

6 cups (48 fl oz/1.5 l) chicken stock

¼ cup (2 fl oz/60 ml) fresh lemon juice

※ In a bowl, combine the meat, onion, rice or bread crumbs, ¼ cup (¼ oz/10 g) of the parsley, the mint or dill and 1 of the eggs. Season to taste with salt and pepper. Using your hands, knead the mixture until well mixed. Form the mixture into tiny meatballs about ½ inch (12 mm) in diameter.

※ In a large saucepan over medium-high heat, bring the stock to a boil. Add the meatballs, reduce the heat to low, cover and simmer gently until the meatballs are cooked, 25–30 minutes.

※ In a bowl, beat the remaining 2 eggs until very frothy. Gradually beat in the lemon juice. Then gradually beat in about 1½ cups (12 fl oz/375 ml)

of the hot soup, beating constantly to prevent curdling. (This step tempers the eggs so that they won't scramble when added to the soup.) Continue to beat until thickened, then slowly stir the egg mixture into the hot soup. Heat through, but do not allow the soup to boil.

※ Ladle into warmed bowls, sprinkle with the remaining ¼ cup (¼ oz/10 g) parsley and serve hot.

Serves 6

Greek Salad

*The simple Greek salad that appears on every taverna table is no culinary groundbreaker.
What makes it so special in Greece is the intense flavor of the local tomatoes and cucumbers,
so use the best-quality produce you can find. In most instances, the salad is dressed simply
with virgin olive oil, but fresh lemon juice or vinegar can also be added.*

DRESSING
½ cup (4 fl oz/125 ml) virgin olive oil
2–3 tablespoons fresh lemon juice
3 tablespoons dried oregano
Freshly cracked pepper
1 clove garlic, finely minced (optional)

2–3 cups (2–3 oz/60–90 g) torn assorted salad greens such as romaine (cos), escarole (Batavian endive) or frisée
4 small ripe tomatoes, cored and cut into wedges
1 large cucumber, peeled, seeded and cut into wedges
1 red (Spanish) onion, thinly sliced into rings
2 small green bell peppers (capsicums), seeded, deribbed and thinly sliced crosswise into rings
½ lb (250 g) feta cheese, coarsely crumbled
20 Kalamata olives

▨ To make the dressing, in a bowl, stir together the olive oil, lemon juice, oregano, cracked pepper to taste, and the garlic, if using. Set aside.

▨ In a large salad bowl, combine the greens, tomatoes, cucumber, onion and bell peppers. Drizzle the dressing over the top and toss gently to mix. Sprinkle the feta cheese and olives over the top and serve.

Serves 4

Spinach with Raisins and Pine Nuts

Although this particular recipe has a Spanish name, you can find similar dishes prepared in Italy, Greece and Turkey. The combination of nuts and dried fruits suggests its Arabic origins. If the spinach leaves are especially large, you may tear or cut them into smaller pieces for faster cooking and easier eating.

¼   cup (1½ oz/45 g) raisins
¼   cup (1 oz/30 g) pine nuts
3   tablespoons olive oil
1   small onion, chopped
2   lb (1 kg) spinach, stems removed and carefully washed
    Salt and freshly ground pepper

❋ Place the raisins in a bowl, add hot water to cover and let stand until plumped, about 20 minutes.

❋ Meanwhile, preheat an oven to 350°F (180°C). Spread the pine nuts in a small pan and place in the oven until toasted and fragrant, 8–10 minutes. Set aside.

❋ In a wide sauté pan over medium heat, warm the olive oil. Add the onion and sauté until tender, about 10 minutes. Add the spinach to the pan and stir constantly until it is wilted, about 4 minutes.

❋ Drain the raisins and add them to the pan along with the pine nuts. Season to taste with salt and pepper, stir well and serve hot.

Serves 4

Sautéed Mushrooms with Garlic

Savor these garlicky sautéed mushrooms hot from the pan. Spoon them over grilled bread as a snack or alongside grilled lamb, beef or chicken as a flavorful side dish. For a particularly delicious variation, combine chanterelles, portobellos and cremini with the more common white mushrooms.

5 tablespoons (2½ fl oz/75 ml) olive oil or equal parts unsalted butter and olive oil

2 tablespoons minced garlic

¼ cup (1½ oz/45 g) diced bacon or cooked diced ham

1 lb (500 g) fresh mushrooms *(see note above),* brushed clean and halved if small or sliced ¼ inch (6 mm) thick

¼ cup (2 fl oz/60 ml) dry white wine or dry sherry, if needed

⅓ cup (½ oz/15 g) chopped fresh flat-leaf (Italian) parsley, or ¼ cup (⅓ oz/10 g) chopped fresh flat-leaf (Italian) parsley and 2 tablespoons chopped fresh thyme

Salt and freshly ground pepper

※ In a large sauté pan over medium heat, warm the olive oil or melt the butter with the olive oil. Add the garlic and bacon or ham and sauté for 2 minutes. Raise the heat to high, add the mushrooms and continue to sauté, stirring briskly, until they release their juices and the liquid evaporates, 5–8 minutes.

If the mushrooms do not release much liquid, add the wine or sherry and cook until the liquid evaporates.

※ Add the parsley or the parsley and thyme and stir well. Season to taste with salt and pepper and serve hot.

Serves 4

Stuffed Eggplant

The name of this famous Turkish eggplant dish means "the imam (priest) fainted," a condition probably brought on by how delicious it is. If possible, prepare this dish from 24–48 hours in advance so the flavors can mellow. If you cannot find Asian or small globe eggplants, you can substitute large globe eggplants by cutting them in half lengthwise and making the slits for stuffing in the cut side.

8   Asian (slender) eggplants or 4 very small globe eggplants (aubergines), about 2 lb (1 kg) total weight
½   cup (4 fl oz/125 ml) olive oil
3   large onions, halved and thinly sliced
2   cups (12 oz/375 g) peeled, seeded and diced tomatoes (fresh or canned)
12   cloves garlic, finely minced
    Salt and freshly ground pepper
    Pinch of sugar
½   cup (¾ oz/20 g) chopped fresh flat-leaf (Italian) parsley
1   cup (8 fl oz/250 ml) hot water

✻ Cut off and discard the stems from the eggplants. Using a sharp knife, peel the eggplants to form a striped pattern that resembles a barber pole.

✻ In a large sauté pan over medium heat, warm the olive oil. Add the eggplants and sauté until tender and softened on all sides, 5–8 minutes for the Asian variety and 15 minutes for the globe variety. Using a slotted spatula or tongs, carefully transfer the eggplants to a baking dish, arranging them side by side.

✻ Add the onions to the oil remaining in the pan and sauté over medium heat until tender, about 8 minutes. Add the tomatoes and garlic and continue to sauté for 2 minutes longer. Season to taste with salt and pepper and add the sugar. Stir in the parsley and set aside.

✻ Preheat an oven to 350°F (180°C).

✻ Cut a lengthwise slit about halfway through each eggplant and to within 1 inch (2.5 cm) of both ends. Carefully pull the slit open to make a pocket. Stuff each slit with an equal amount of the tomato-onion mixture. Add the hot water to the pan, cover with aluminum foil and bake until the eggplants are very tender when pierced with a fork, 15–20 minutes for the Asian variety and 30–45 minutes for the globe variety.

✻ Transfer the eggplants to a platter. Let cool. Serve at room temperature.

Serves 4

City–Style Braised Artichokes

Despite its Greek name, this delicious ragout is believed to have originated in Istanbul, and both the Turks and Greeks claim it as their own. Peas or favas may be added to the mixture. If adding favas, immerse the shelled beans in boiling water for 1 minute, then drain and peel off their skins.

Juice of 2 lemons, plus fresh lemon juice to taste, optional

3 tablespoons all-purpose (plain) flour

6 large artichokes with 1–2 inches (2.5–5 cm) of stem intact

½ cup (4 fl oz/125 ml) olive oil

1 yellow onion, chopped

8 green (spring) onions, coarsely chopped

3 carrots, peeled and diced

2 large white boiling potatoes, cut into 1-inch (2.5-cm) dice, or 6–8 tiny new potatoes, halved

1 cup (5 oz/155 g) shelled peas or shelled and peeled fava (broad) beans (optional; *see note above*)

Salt and freshly ground pepper

½ cup (¾ oz/20 g) chopped fresh dill

❈ Fill a large bowl with cold water and add the juice of 2 lemons and the flour. Snap off the tough outer leaves from the artichokes. Using a paring knife, trim the dark green parts from the base and stem. Cut the artichokes lengthwise into quarters and scoop out and discard the prickly chokes. As they are cut, drop the artichoke quarters into the bowl of lemon water to prevent discoloring until they are needed.

❈ In a large sauté pan over medium heat, warm the olive oil. Add the onion and sauté until softened, about 2 minutes. Add the green onions and carrots and sauté until tender, about 5 minutes longer.

❈ Drain the artichokes and add to the pan along with the unpeeled potatoes and enough hot water to cover the vegetables. Cover and cook over low heat until the potatoes and artichokes are tender, about 25 minutes. If using peas or favas, add them during the last 10–15 minutes of cooking.

❈ Season to taste with salt and pepper and some lemon juice, if desired. Transfer to a serving dish and let cool. Sprinkle with the dill and serve at room temperature.

Serves 4–6

Rice Pilaf with Pine Nuts and Currants

Simple rice pilafs like this one often accompany kebabs or vegetarian dishes in tavernas throughout the Mediterranean. Fragrant basmati rice is a particularly good choice for this dish, as each grain holds its shape and resists gumminess. If sautéed chicken livers are added, the dish is known as ic pilav.

2   cups (14 oz/440 g) long-grain white rice, preferably basmati

2   teaspoons salt, plus salt to taste

4   cups (32 fl oz/1 l) boiling water

4   chicken livers, optional

2   tablespoons plus ¼ cup (2 oz/60 g) unsalted butter

1   onion, chopped

3   tablespoons pine nuts

½   teaspoon ground cinnamon or ground allspice

3   cups (24 fl oz/750 ml) chicken stock or equal parts chicken stock and water

¼   cup (1½ oz/45 g) dried currants
    Freshly ground pepper

3   tablespoons chopped fresh flat-leaf (Italian) parsley or dill

※ In a bowl, combine the rice with the 2 teaspoons salt and pour in the boiling water. Stir well and let stand until the water is cold.

※ Meanwhile, if using the chicken livers, in a small sauté pan over medium-high heat, melt the 2 tablespoons butter. Add the livers and sauté until browned and firm but still pink in the center, about 5 minutes. Let cool, then chop coarsely. Set aside.

※ Drain the rice and rinse well under cool running water. Drain again and set aside.

※ In a saucepan over medium heat, melt the ¼ cup (2 oz/60 g) butter. Add the onion and pine nuts and sauté until pale golden brown, about 8 minutes. Add the rice and cook, stirring, until opaque, about 5 minutes. Add the cinnamon or allspice,

the stock or stock and water, currants and chicken livers, if using. Season to taste with salt and pepper. Cover and cook over medium-low heat until the liquid is absorbed, about 15 minutes.

※ Uncover the pan, drape a folded kitchen towel over the pan and replace the lid. Cook over very low heat for 10 minutes longer. Turn off the heat and let stand for 15 minutes before serving. Sprinkle with the parsley or dill and serve.

Serves 4

Eggplant and Tomato Pilaf

This flavorful pilaf can become the centerpiece of a meal as easily as it can be a side dish. The tomatoes lend a lovely pink to the rice. Accompany the pilaf with cooked greens and yogurt-cucumber sauce (recipe on page 13) or plain yogurt.

2   eggplants (aubergines), about 3 lb (1.5 kg) total weight
2   cups (14 oz/440 g) long-grain white rice, preferably basmati
2   teaspoons salt, plus salt to taste
4   cups (32 fl oz/1 l) boiling water
1   cup (8 fl oz/250 ml) olive oil, or as needed
1   onion, chopped
2   large tomatoes, peeled, seeded and chopped
½   teaspoon ground cinnamon
½   teaspoon ground allspice
1   teaspoon freshly ground pepper
2   cups (16 fl oz/500 ml) hot water or tomato juice
    Chopped fresh mint

❊ Peel the eggplants and cut into ½-inch (12-mm) cubes. Place the cubes in a colander, salt lightly and toss gently to mix. Let stand for about 1 hour to drain off the bitter juices.

❊ Meanwhile, in a bowl, combine the rice with the 2 teaspoons salt and pour in the boiling water. Stir well and let stand until the water is cold. Drain the rice and rinse well under cool running water. Drain again and set aside.

❊ Rinse the eggplant cubes with cool water, drain well and pat dry with paper towels.

❊ In a large sauté pan over medium-high heat, warm 3 tablespoons of the olive oil. Working in 3 batches and adding 3 tablespoons olive oil with each batch, add the eggplant cubes and sauté until golden brown on all sides, about 5 minutes. Using a slotted spoon, transfer the cubes to paper towels to drain and set aside.

❊ In a saucepan over medium heat, warm the remaining 3 tablespoons olive oil. Add the onion and sauté until tender, about 8 minutes. Add the rice and cook, stirring, until opaque, about 3 minutes. Add the tomatoes and cook, stirring, for 5 minutes longer. Add the sautéed eggplant, cinnamon, allspice, salt to taste and pepper and stir well. Pour in the hot water or tomato juice, cover and cook over low heat until the liquid is absorbed, 15–20 minutes.

❊ Uncover the pan, drape a folded kitchen towel over the rim and replace the lid. Let stand for 15–20 minutes before serving. Sprinkle with mint and serve.

Serves 4

Fish and Shellfish

No matter where you are in the Mediterranean, the sea or a freshwater stream is never far away. So it comes as no surprise that fish and shellfish appear in abundance on the taverna table. Invariably they are served fresh from the waters, and they are usually grilled or fried and occasionally baked, braised or poached.

Because freshness is a given, lengthy marinades and complex sauces are seldom part of the preparation. Lemon wedges are the most common garnish, serving to heighten the scent of the sea, and most sauces—*romesco, tarator, skordalia, piri-piri*—are placed on the side, to be used as an accent and not a disguise.

Fish may be wrapped in grape leaves or a thin slice of cured ham before grilling, or threaded onto skewers with fresh bay leaves and slivers of onion. If fish is marinated at all, it is for a short time in an understated mixture of olive oil, lemon juice and and one or two carefully chosen herbs or spices. And if cooked in a sauce, it is always a simple one, perhaps combining just tomato, garlic, onion and a splash of wine.

AMÊIJOAS NA CATAPLANA – PORTUGAL

Stewed Clams with Sausage, Ham and Tomatoes

The name for this dish from the Algarve comes from the clam-shaped copper cooking vessel, known as a cataplana, *in which it is classically cooked. Serve this popular* tasca *dish as a light supper or lunch, accompanied with lots of bread for soaking up any extra juices, or spoon it over rice or alongside boiled potatoes for a more substantial main course. Serve chili pepper sauce (recipe on page 15) on the side.*

- 2½ lb (1.25 kg) small clams in the shell such as Manilas
- 2 tablespoons olive oil
- 3 yellow or red (Spanish) onions, thinly sliced
- 4 cloves garlic, finely minced
- 1½ tablespoons red pepper flakes or 2 fresh small hot chili peppers, seeded and finely chopped (optional)
- 1 bay leaf, crumbled
- ¼ lb (125 g) smoked ham or prosciutto, diced
- ¼ lb (125 g) *chouriço* sausage, casing removed and crumbled
- ½ cup (4 fl oz/125 ml) dry white wine
- 2 cups (12 oz/375 g) diced canned tomatoes and their juices
- ½ cup (¾ oz/20 g) chopped fresh flat-leaf (Italian) parsley
- Freshly ground black pepper
- Lemon wedges

Discard any clams that do not close to the touch. Scrub the clams well under running water, place in a bowl of water, and refrigerate until needed.

In a large sauté pan over medium heat, warm the olive oil. Add the onions and sauté until tender, about 8 minutes. Add the garlic and the red pepper flakes, if using, and sauté for 3 minutes longer. Add the fresh chilies (if using), the bay leaf, ham or prosciutto, sausage, wine and tomatoes. Stir well and simmer over low heat, uncovered, for 25 minutes.

Add the clams, hinge sides down, and cover the pan. Raise the heat to high and cook until the clams open, 3–5 minutes. Discard any clams that have not opened.

Ladle into warmed soup bowls, sprinkle with parsley and top with a liberal grinding of black pepper. Serve hot with lemon wedges.

Serves 4

Shrimp with Tomatoes, Oregano and Feta

This dish is served at seaside tavernas all over Greece. The shrimp can be sautéed and dressed with the tomato sauce up to 4 hours in advance. At serving time, sprinkle on the feta cheese and slip under a broiler or into an oven. Serve with plenty of crusty bread for capturing the delicious juices.

1½   lb (750 g) large shrimp (prawns), peeled and deveined
Salt and freshly ground black pepper

4   tablespoons (2 fl oz/60 ml) olive oil

1   small yellow onion, chopped, or 6 green (spring) onions, chopped

4   cloves garlic, finely minced
Pinch of ground cayenne pepper, optional

2   tablespoons dried oregano

1½   cups (12 fl oz/375 ml) tomato sauce or 4 large tomatoes, peeled, seeded and diced
Pinch of sugar, if needed

½   lb (250 g) feta cheese, crumbled

¼   cup (⅓ oz/10 g) chopped fresh flat-leaf (Italian) parsley

✵ Preheat an oven to 450°F (230°C) or preheat a broiler (griller).

✵ Sprinkle the shrimp with salt and black pepper. In a large sauté pan over medium-high heat, warm 2 tablespoons of the olive oil. Add the shrimp and sauté, stirring briskly, until pink and beginning to curl, 2–3 minutes. Using a slotted spoon, transfer the shrimp to 4 flameproof ramekins or small gratin dishes, distributing them evenly.

✵ In the same pan over medium heat, warm the remaining 2 tablespoons olive oil. Add the yellow onion or green onions and sauté until tender, about 8 minutes. Add the garlic, cayenne (if using), and oregano and sauté for 2 minutes longer. Add the tomato sauce or diced tomatoes and simmer until thickened slightly, about 2 minutes longer. Add the sugar if the tomatoes are not sweet and season to taste with salt and black pepper.

✵ Pour the sauce over the shrimp, dividing it evenly. Then sprinkle the feta over the tops. Bake or broil until the cheese melts, 5–8 minutes if baking or 3–5 minutes if broiling.

✵ Sprinkle the shrimp with the parsley and serve hot.

Serves 4

Fish in Grape Leaves

Cooking fish in grape leaves is an ancient Mediterranean tradition. Whole large sardines and tiny red mullets are among the most popular choices, although fish fillets can also be adapted to this method of cooking. In place of the lemon wedges, you can make a simple dressing of 5 tablespoons olive oil, 2–3 tablespoons fresh lemon juice and a complementary herb of your choice.

¼ cup (2 fl oz/60 ml) olive oil

2 tablespoons chopped fresh flat-leaf (Italian) parsley or fennel fronds

2 teaspoons chopped fresh thyme or dried oregano
Juice of 1 lemon
Salt and freshly ground pepper

2 lb (1 kg) fresh large sardines, cleaned with heads left on, or 4 fish fillets such as sea bass, cod or sole, about 6 oz (185 g) each
Bottled grape leaves, rinsed of brine and stems removed
Lemon wedges

※ In a large, shallow nonaluminum dish, whisk together the olive oil, parsley or fennel, thyme or oregano, lemon juice and season to taste with salt and pepper. Add the fish and turn to coat well. Let marinate at room temperature for about 1 hour.

※ Preheat a broiler (griller) or prepare a fire in a charcoal grill. Using 1 or 2 grape leaves per whole fish or fillet, wrap the leaves around the center, leaving exposed the head and tail of each fish or both ends of each fillet; secure the leaves with toothpicks, if needed.

※ Place the fish packets on a broiler pan or an oiled grill rack and broil or grill, turning once, until opaque throughout, 7–10 minutes per side for whole fish and 5–6 minutes per side for fish fillets.

※ Transfer to a warmed platter and serve hot with lemon wedges.

Serves 4

Gratin of Salt Cod and Potatoes

Gomes de Sá was a well-regarded restaurateur from the city of Porto, and this dish, one of his specialties, has become a permanent part of the sizable Portuguese repertoire of salt cod recipes. This bacalhau classic can be assembled up to 8 hours in advance and then reheated in the oven just before serving time.

1	lb (500 g) skinless salt cod fillets
	Hot milk, if needed
1½	lb (750 g) boiling potatoes (about 3 large), peeled
6	tablespoons (3 fl oz/90 ml) olive oil
2	onions, thinly sliced
2	cloves garlic, minced (optional)
½	cup (¾ oz/20 g) chopped fresh flat-leaf (Italian) parsley
1	teaspoon freshly ground pepper
20	oil-cured black olives
2	eggs, hard-cooked and sliced

Place the salt cod in a bowl and add cold water to cover. Cover and refrigerate for 24–48 hours, changing the water often.

Drain the cod well, rinse in cold water and place in a saucepan. Add water to cover and slowly bring to a gentle boil. Reduce the heat to low and simmer gently until the cod is tender when pierced with a fork and flakes easily, 15–20 minutes.

Drain the cod and let cool. Using your fingers, break up the cod, removing any errant bones, skin or tough parts. Taste it. If it seems too salty, place in a bowl, add hot milk to cover and let stand for 30 minutes, then drain.

Place the potatoes in a saucepan and add water to cover. Bring to a boil over high heat and boil until cooked through but still firm when pierced with a fork, 10–15 minutes. Drain well and when cool enough to handle, cut into slices ¼ inch (6 mm) thick. Set aside.

In a large sauté pan over medium heat, warm 2 tablespoons of the olive oil. Add the onions and sauté until tender but not browned, about 8 minutes.

Add the garlic, if using, and sauté for 2 minutes longer. Using a slotted spoon, transfer to a plate and set aside.

In the same pan over medium heat, warm 3 tablespoons of the olive oil. Add the potatoes and sauté, stirring briskly, until golden, 5–8 minutes. Remove from the heat.

Preheat an oven to 400°F (200°C). Oil an 11-by-7-by-1½-inch (28-by-18-by-4-cm) oval gratin dish or 4 individual gratin dishes. Layer half of the potatoes in the dish or dishes. Top with half of the cod, then half of the onions and parsley. Sprinkle with the pepper. Repeat the layering with the remaining potatoes, cod and onions. Drizzle with the remaining 1 tablespoon olive oil.

Bake until golden, about 25 minutes. Garnish with the olives and hard-cooked eggs, sprinkle with the remaining parsley and serve.

Serves 4

KILIC SIS KEBAP – TURKEY

Grilled Swordfish Kebabs

One of the simplest and best fish recipes of the Turkish Aegean, these flavorful kebabs are equally popular in Greece. If the cherry tomatoes are not firm, skewer them separately and remove them from the heat as soon as they are done. Dress the brochettes with a vinaigrette of olive oil and lemon juice or serve with nut sauce (recipe on page 30). Rice pilaf (page 62) is the classic accompaniment.

- ½ cup (4 fl oz/125 ml) olive oil
- 6 tablespoons (3 fl oz/90 ml) fresh lemon juice
- 1 teaspoon paprika
- 2 bay leaves, crushed, plus 12 whole bay leaves
- 2 lb (1 kg) swordfish fillets, cut into 1¼-inch (3-cm) cubes
- 2 lemons, thinly sliced, plus lemon wedges for serving
- 2 green bell peppers (capsicums), seeded, deribbed and cut into 1¼-inch (3-cm) squares
- 16 ripe but firm cherry tomatoes
- Salt and freshly ground pepper

In a shallow nonaluminum bowl, whisk together the olive oil, lemon juice, paprika and crushed bay leaves. Add the swordfish cubes, turning to coat well. Cover and let marinate in the refrigerator for about 4 hours.

Prepare a fire in a charcoal grill or preheat a broiler (griller).

Remove the fish cubes from the marinade, reserving the marinade. Thread the cubes onto metal skewers, alternating them with the whole bay leaves, lemon slices, bell peppers and cherry tomatoes. Sprinkle with salt and pepper.

Place the skewers on an oiled grill rack or a broiler pan and grill or broil, turning as needed and basting a few times with the reserved marinade, until the fish is opaque throughout, about 10 minutes.

Transfer the skewers to a warmed platter and serve hot with lemon wedges.

Serves 4

PESCADO EN PICADA – SPAIN

Fish in Almond Sauce

This simple taberna *dish features the classic Catalan nut sauce known as* picada. *With its heady mixture of nuts, bread and garlic,* picada *is evidence of the Arabic influence in Spanish cooking.* Merluza *(hake) is traditionally used in this dish, but you may substitute cod, sea bass, flounder or other firm white fish.*

ALMOND SAUCE

- ½ cup (2½ oz/75 g) slivered blanched almonds
- 2 tablespoons olive oil
- 1 large onion, finely chopped
- 1 teaspoon paprika
- 1 tablespoon finely minced garlic
- ¼ cup (½ oz/15 g) fresh bread crumbs
- Pinch of saffron threads, crushed (optional)
- 1½ cups (9 oz/280 g) peeled, seeded and diced tomatoes (fresh or canned)
- 1 cup (8 fl oz/250 ml) fish stock or dry white wine
- Salt and freshly ground pepper
- 1 cup (5 oz/155 g) shelled peas, optional
- 4 firm white fish fillets, each about 5 oz (155 g) *(see note above)*
- Salt and freshly ground pepper
- ¼ cup (⅓ oz/10 g) chopped fresh flat-leaf (Italian) parsley or mint

To make the almond sauce, preheat an oven to 350°F (180°C). Spread the almonds on a baking sheet and place in the oven until toasted and fragrant, 8–10 minutes. Let cool.

Place ¼ cup (1¼ oz/37 g) of the almonds aside to use for garnish. Using a food processor fitted with the metal blade or a nut grinder, finely grind the remaining almonds, being careful not to overgrind to a paste. Set the ground nuts aside.

In a sauté pan over medium heat, warm the olive oil. Add the onion and sauté until tender but not browned, about 8 minutes. Add the paprika, garlic, ground almonds, bread crumbs and the saffron, if using, and sauté for 3 minutes longer. Add the tomatoes and stock or wine and cook over medium heat, stirring occasionally, until slightly thickened, 5–8 minutes. Season to taste with salt and pepper. Remove from the heat and set aside.

If using the peas, bring a saucepan three-fourths full of water to a boil. Add the peas and boil until barely tender, 3–6 minutes.

Raise the oven temperature to 450°F (230°C). Sprinkle the fillets on both sides with salt and pepper and place in a single layer in a baking dish. Spoon the sauce over the fish, add the peas, if using, and bake in the oven until the fish is opaque throughout, 10–12 minutes. Garnish with the reserved toasted almonds and the parsley or mint. Serve at once.

Serves 4

Stuffed Squid

Different variations on stuffed squid are found on taverna tables in Greece and Portugal as well as Spain. The squid are sometimes served atop a bed of wilted assorted greens, such as dandelion, escarole (Batavian endive), kale, arugula (rocket) and chicory (curly endive).

12	medium or 16 small squid

BREAD CRUMB FILLING

3	tablespoons olive oil
1½	cups (6 oz/185 g) chopped onion
4	cloves garlic, minced
½	cup (3 oz/90 g) chopped serrano, prosciutto or similar cured ham (optional)
1–1½	cups (2–3 oz/60–90 g) fresh bread crumbs
¼	cup (2 fl oz/60 ml) fresh lemon juice
6	tablespoons (⅓ oz/10 g) chopped fresh flat-leaf (Italian) parsley
	Salt and freshly ground pepper
	Olive oil for brushing
	Salt and freshly ground pepper

OLIVE OIL DRESSING

⅓	cup (3 fl oz/80 ml) virgin olive oil
3–4	tablespoons fresh lemon juice
3	tablespoons dried oregano

※ To clean each squid, grip the head and pull it and the attached innards gently but firmly from the body. Using your fingertips, squeeze out the small, round beak from the mouth at the base of the tentacles. Using a sharp knife, cut away the eyes, reserving the tentacles. Using your fingers, clean out the body pouch under running water, being careful not to tear it. Remove and discard the transparent quill-like cartilage from along one side of the pouch. Rub off the filmy brownish skin from the body and rinse the tentacles and body well. Chop the tentacles and set the bodies and tentacles aside.

※ Preheat a broiler (griller) or prepare a fire in a charcoal grill.

※ To make the bread crumb filling, in a sauté pan over medium heat, warm the olive oil. Add the onion and sauté until tender, 8–10 minutes.

※ Add the garlic, ham (if using), chopped tentacles and enough of the bread crumbs to bind the mixture together. Sauté over medium heat for 2 minutes. Stir in the lemon juice and parsley and season to taste with salt and pepper. Let cool.

※ Carefully stuff the bread crumb mixture into the squid bodies and skewer the ends closed with toothpicks. Thread the squid crosswise onto long metal skewers. Brush them with olive oil and sprinkle with salt and pepper. Place on a broiler pan or a grill rack and broil or grill, turning once, until the squid are tender and opaque, about 3 minutes per side.

※ Meanwhile, make the dressing: In a small bowl, whisk together the virgin olive oil, lemon juice and oregano.

※ Slide the squid off the skewers onto a warmed platter, drizzle the dressing evenly over the top and serve hot.

Serves 4

Trout Wrapped in Ham

This savory fish dish, from the region of Navarra in the northeast, is one of the best-known preparations for trout in all of Spain. Although often accompanied with just boiled potatoes and a squeeze of lemon, the trout is also frequently served with a topping of sautéed mushrooms, given as an option below.

4   freshwater trout, cleaned with heads intact, each about ¾ lb (375 g)
    Salt and freshly ground pepper
8   thin slices serrano, prosciutto or similar cured ham
    About 1 cup (5 oz/155 g) all-purpose (plain) flour
⅓   cup (3 fl oz/80 ml) olive oil

MUSHROOM TOPPING (OPTIONAL)
¼   cup (2 fl oz/60 ml) dry white wine
2   tablespoons unsalted butter
1½ cups (4½ oz/140 g) sliced fresh mushrooms

    Lemon wedges

❁ Sprinkle the trout inside and out with salt and pepper. Slip 1 slice of ham inside each trout. Wrap a second ham slice around the center of each trout, leaving the head and tail exposed. Skewer the cavity closed with toothpicks or tie with kitchen string. Spread the flour on a large plate.

❁ In a large sauté pan or frying pan over medium heat, warm the olive oil. Dip the trout in the flour, coating it evenly, and fry, turning once, until golden on both sides, about 4 minutes per side. Transfer to a warmed platter or individual plates.

❁ If a mushroom topping is desired, raise the heat to high, pour the wine into the pan and deglaze the pan by stirring to dislodge any browned bits from the pan bottom. Reduce the heat to medium, add the butter and when it melts, add the mushrooms. Sauté until tender, about 8 minutes.

❁ Remove the toothpicks or string from the trout and spoon the mushrooms over them, if using. Serve hot with lemon wedges.

Serves 4

Paella

*Taking its name from the shallow, two-handled metal pan in which it is traditionally
cooked, paella can be as simple or as extravagant as time and money permit. Paella originated
in Valencia, although many regions of Spain have their own special variations.*

24 small clams in the shell
24 mussels in the shell
1 chicken, 3 lb (1.5 kg), cut into serving pieces
 Salt and freshly ground pepper
 Olive oil
½ lb (250 g) chorizo sausages
1 lb (500 g) medium shrimp (prawns), peeled and deveined
2 onions, chopped
6 cloves garlic, finely minced
2 red or green bell peppers (capsicums), seeded, deribbed and diced
1½ cups (9 oz/280 g) peeled, seeded and diced tomatoes (fresh or canned)
3 cups (21 oz/655 g) short-grain white rice
6 cups (48 fl oz/1.5 l) chicken stock
¼ teaspoon saffron threads, crushed with a mortar and pestle
1 cup (5 oz/155 g) shelled peas, shelled and peeled fava (broad) beans, or lima beans
 Lemon wedges
 Strips of roasted and peeled pimiento pepper (capsicum), optional

❊ Discard any clams or mussels that do not close to the touch. Scrub them well under running water and pull the beards from the mussels. Place the clams in a bowl of water and the mussels in a dry bowl and store in the refrigerator until needed.

❊ Rinse the chicken pieces and pat dry. Sprinkle with salt and pepper to taste. Place a large, deep sauté pan over high heat and pour in enough olive oil to film the pan bottom lightly. Add the chicken and brown well on all sides, 8–10 minutes. Using tongs or a slotted spoon, transfer the chicken to a plate; set aside.

❊ If needed, pour a little more olive oil into the oil remaining in the pan and place over medium-high heat. Add the sausages and cook, turning, until firm and browned on all sides, about 5–8 minutes. Using the tongs or slotted spoon, transfer the sausages to the plate with the chicken. Cut the sausages into chunks and set aside.

❊ Add the shrimp to the same pan and sauté over medium-high heat, stirring briskly, until pink and beginning to curl, 2–3 minutes. Again, transfer with the tongs or slotted spoon to the plate holding the other ingredients.

❊ Add the onions to the oil remaining in the pan and sauté over medium heat until softened, 5–6 minutes, adding a little more olive oil if needed to prevent scorching. Add the garlic and bell peppers and sauté until beginning to soften, about 5 minutes longer. Add the tomatoes and cook, stirring, for 3 minutes longer. Stir in the rice, pour in the chicken stock and add the saffron. Bring to a boil, then reduce the heat to low and simmer, uncovered, for 10 minutes.

❊ Add the browned chicken and sausages and the peas or beans, pushing them into the rice slightly, and simmer, uncovered, for 10 minutes.

❊ Drain the clams. Scatter the clams, mussels and the reserved shrimp over the top, cover and cook until the clams and mussels open, 4–5 minutes. Discard any clams and mussels that have not opened.

❊ Remove from the heat and let stand for a few minutes until most of the liquid is absorbed and the rice is tender. Serve directly from the pan or spoon onto individual plates. Garnish with lemon wedges and strips of pimiento, if using.

Serves 4–6

84

Poultry and Meat

Fresh meat and poultry have not always been a daily feature on taverna menus. In the past, meat was used sparingly, usually offered in small portions or to enhance the flavor of a soup, pilaf or bean ragout. But, as the prosperity of the region has grown, meat and poultry dishes have become more common menu items.

Stews make up a large part of the repertoire, as do meats and small birds cooked over an open flame. The aromas rising from a kitchen grill or rotisserie frequently offer the first tantalizing greeting to customers as they pass through the doors of a taverna. Portions are often smaller than those customarily served in America or Europe. A skewer with just a few pieces of meat is a typical serving, and diners are expected to round out their meals with vegetables, a pilaf or potatoes and bread.

Lamb and pork are the most popular meats, and the animals are routinely eaten when very young. Although a lamb chop may be just a bite or two and the leg but a few pounds, the meat is exceptionally sweet and uncommonly tender. Both meat and poultry, which is generally free-range, often require only a few fresh herb sprigs or a simple marinade and a squeeze or two of lemon to highlight their full, natural flavors.

87

Grilled Chicken Kebabs

The yogurt in this classic marinade tenderizes the chicken, yielding succulent results. If you like, grill vegetables on separate skewers so their cooking can be easily monitored. Serve the kebabs with pita bread or pilaf and spoon some yogurt-cucumber sauce (recipe on page 13) over the grilled vegetables.

1	large yellow onion, chopped
4	cloves garlic, minced
¼	cup (2 fl oz/60 ml) fresh lemon juice
1	tablespoon paprika
½	teaspoon ground cayenne pepper
½	teaspoon freshly ground black pepper, plus pepper to taste
1	tablespoon chopped fresh thyme
1	cup (8 oz/250 g) plain yogurt
1½	lb (750 g) boneless, skinless chicken breasts or thighs
	Olive oil for brushing
	Salt

In a food processor fitted with the metal blade or in a blender, combine the onion, garlic, lemon juice, paprika, cayenne, the ½ teaspoon black pepper and the thyme. Use rapid on-off pulses to combine well. Add the yogurt and pulse to mix.

Rinse the chicken and pat dry. Cut into 1-inch (2.5-cm) cubes and place in a nonaluminum container. Pour the yogurt mixture over the chicken and turn to coat. Cover and let marinate in the refrigerator for 8 hours.

Prepare a fire in a charcoal grill or preheat a broiler (griller).

Remove the chicken pieces from the marinade, reserving the marinade, and thread them onto metal skewers.

Brush the chicken with olive oil and then sprinkle with salt and pepper.

Place the skewers on an oiled grill rack or a broiler pan and grill or broil, turning and basting once with the reserved marinade, until no longer pink in the center when cut into with a knife, 4–5 minutes per side for breast meat and 5–6 minutes per side for thigh meat.

Transfer the skewers to warmed individual plates or a platter. Serve hot.

Serves 4

Chicken with Eggplant, Peppers and Tomatoes

Like ratatouille, samfaina is a mixture of onions, garlic, eggplant, peppers and tomatoes cooked down to a fragrant and unctuous stew. It makes a wonderful addition to a tortilla (recipe on page 22) and is a good sauce for fish. Serve with rice, mashed potatoes or slices of grilled bread.

1   frying chicken, about 4 lb (2 kg), cut into serving pieces
     Salt and freshly ground pepper

¼   cup (2 fl oz/60 ml) olive oil

¼   lb (125 g) diced cooked ham or cured ham such as serrano or prosciutto, optional

2   large onions, sliced or coarsely chopped

1   lb (500 g) Asian (slender) eggplants (aubergines), unpeeled, or 1 globe eggplant, about 1 lb (500 g), peeled

3   cloves garlic, minced

¾   lb (375 g) zucchini (courgettes), cut into ½-inch (12-mm) chunks

2   green or red bell peppers (capsicums), seeded, deribbed and cut lengthwise into strips ½ inch (12 mm) wide

1½   lb (750 g) tomatoes, peeled, seeded and chopped (fresh or canned)

1   bay leaf

2   tablespoons chopped fresh thyme, oregano or marjoram

½   cup (4 fl oz/125 ml) dry white wine

※ Rinse the chicken pieces and pat dry. Sprinkle with salt and pepper.

※ In a large sauté pan over medium-high heat, warm the olive oil. Add the chicken and brown on all sides, about 8 minutes. Using tongs or a slotted spoon, transfer to a plate.

※ To the oil remaining in the pan, add the ham, if using, and sauté over medium heat for 1 minute. Add the onions and sauté until tender and translucent, about 10 minutes.

※ Cut the eggplant(s) into 1-inch (2.5-cm) cubes and add to the onions along with the garlic, zucchini and bell peppers. Sauté until beginning to soften, about 5 minutes longer.

※ Add the tomatoes, bay leaf, thyme or other herb and wine and stir well. Return the chicken to the pan and turn the pieces to mix evenly with the *samfaina*. Cover and simmer over low heat until the chicken is tender and opaque throughout, 25–35 minutes. Discard the bay leaf and season to taste with salt and pepper.

※ Transfer to a warmed serving dish and serve hot.

Serves 4

Roast Chicken with Oregano and Lemon

When Greek cooks roast chicken, more likely than not they will produce this venerable taverna dish, in which the accompanying potatoes become especially tender, juicy and lemony. Serve with white wine and a zesty Greek salad (recipe on page 53), if you like.

1   roasting chicken, about 5 lb (2.5 kg)

1   lemon, quartered

½   cup (4 fl oz/125 ml) olive oil
Salt to taste, plus 1 teaspoon salt
Freshly ground pepper

12 cloves garlic, crushed

2   teaspoons plus 3 tablespoons dried oregano

⅓   cup (3 fl oz/80 ml) fresh lemon juice

2   teaspoons coarsely cracked pepper

6   white boiling potatoes, peeled and cut into large wedges

1   cup (8 fl oz/250 ml) water or chicken stock, or as needed

¼   cup (⅓ oz/10 g) chopped fresh flat-leaf (Italian) parsley

❋ Preheat an oven to 400°F (200°C).

❋ Rinse the chicken and pat dry. Rub the chicken inside and out with the cut lemon quarters, 1–2 tablespoons of the olive oil and sprinkle with salt and ground pepper. Place the lemon quarters, 4 of the garlic cloves and the 2 teaspoons oregano in the chicken cavity. Place the chicken on a rack in a roasting pan.

❋ In a small saucepan, combine the remaining olive oil, the lemon juice, 2 tablespoons of the oregano, the coarsely cracked pepper and the 1 teaspoon salt and bring to a simmer over medium heat. Simmer for 3 minutes to blend the flavors. Remove from the heat and set aside.

❋ Place the potatoes around the chicken and sprinkle them with the remaining 1 tablespoon oregano and the remaining 8 garlic cloves. Spoon a little of the simmered lemon-oil mixture over the chicken. Pour 1 cup (8 fl oz/250 ml) water or stock evenly over the potatoes and place in the oven. Roast for 15 minutes. Baste the chicken with some of the lemon-oil mixture and reduce the heat to 350°F (180°C). Roast the chicken, basting with the lemon-oil mixture every 10–15 minutes, until the juices run clear when the thigh joint is pierced or an instant-read thermometer inserted in the thickest portion of the thigh away from the bone registers 165°F (74°C), about 1 hour.

❋ Transfer the chicken to a warmed platter. If the potatoes aren't golden brown, raise the heat to 450°F (230°C) and cook for 15–20 minutes longer, adding more water or stock if needed to prevent sticking.

❋ Arrange the potatoes alongside the chicken. Using a large spoon, skim off the fat from the roasting pan, then pour the pan juices into a serving container. Sprinkle the chicken and potatoes with the parsley. Carve the chicken and pass the pan juices at the table.

Serves 4

Sausage and Green Pepper Ragout

This rustic stew of sausages and sweet green peppers is a specialty of the villages on Mount Pelion in central Greece. The traditional loukanika *sausage is subtly seasoned with orange zest, marjoram, coriander and allspice. You may want to add a bit of these aromatics to the stew if you can find only Italian sausage. Serve with simmered white beans or crusty bread.*

4   tablespoons (2 fl oz/60 ml) olive oil

1   lb (500 g) Greek *loukanika* or Italian sweet sausages, sliced ¾ inch (2 cm) thick

1   lb (500 g) long sweet green peppers (capsicums), seeded, deribbed and cut lengthwise into strips 1 inch (2.5 cm) wide

1   lb (500 g) tomatoes, peeled, seeded and chopped (fresh or canned)

1   tablespoon dried oregano

¼   teaspoon ground allspice, optional

½   teaspoon ground coriander, optional

2   teaspoons grated orange zest, optional

   Salt and freshly ground pepper

※ In a large sauté pan over high heat, warm 2 tablespoons of the olive oil. Add the sausages and brown on all sides, about 5 minutes. Using a slotted spoon, transfer the sausages to a plate and set aside.

※ Add the remaining 2 tablespoons oil to the pan. Then add the sweet peppers and sauté over medium heat until softened, 5–8 minutes.

※ Return the sausages to the pan and add the tomatoes, oregano and, if using Italian sausage, add the allspice, coriander and orange zest. Cover and simmer over low heat until the flavors have blended and the sauce has thickened, 15–20 minutes.

※ Season the ragout to taste with salt and pepper. Transfer to a warmed serving dish and serve hot.

Serves 4

Grilled Meatballs

Quintessential taverna fare, these flavorful meatballs—Turkey's answer to American hamburgers—are grilled quickly over charcoal, then served tucked into warm pita bread with sliced tomatoes and onions and a garlicky yogurt sauce. The onions are traditionally flavored with sumac, a slightly sour, peppery ground spice used in many Middle Eastern cuisines.

YOGURT SAUCE
4   cups (32 oz/1 kg) plain yogurt
3   large cloves garlic, finely minced
3   tablespoons olive oil
1   tablespoon red wine vinegar or fresh lemon juice, or to taste
¼   cup (⅓ oz/10 g) chopped fresh mint
Salt and freshly ground pepper

ONION SALAD
1   lb (500 g) red (Spanish) or white onions
1   tablespoon salt
½   cup (¾ oz/20 g) chopped fresh flat-leaf (Italian) parsley
1   teaspoon sumac, optional

MEATBALLS
2   lb (1 kg) ground (minced) lean lamb or beef
2   yellow or red (Spanish) onions, grated (about 1½ cups/7½ oz/235 g)
2   cloves garlic, finely minced
2   eggs
1   tablespoon chopped fresh thyme
1   teaspoon freshly ground pepper
½   teaspoon salt, plus salt to taste
Olive oil for brushing

6 pita breads, warmed

To make the yogurt sauce, line a large sieve with cheesecloth (muslin), place it over a bowl and spoon the yogurt into the sieve. Refrigerate for 4–6 hours to drain off the excess water. You should have 1½–2 cups (12–16 oz/375–500 g) drained yogurt. Add the garlic, olive oil and vinegar or lemon juice to the drained yogurt. Stir well and fold in the mint. Season to taste with salt and pepper. Cover and refrigerate until needed.

Prepare a fire in a charcoal grill or preheat a broiler (griller).

To make the onion salad, cut any large onions in half and then thinly slice all of the onions. Place the onion slices in a large sieve or colander, add the salt and toss well. Let stand for 15 minutes. Rinse the onion slices with cool water and pat dry with paper towels. Place in a bowl and add the parsley and the sumac, if using. Toss well and set aside.

To make the meatballs, in a bowl, combine the lamb or beef, grated onions, garlic, eggs, thyme, pepper and the ½ teaspoon salt. Mix with your hands until the mixture holds together well. Form into 12 ovals about 3 inches (7.5 cm) long and 1½ inches (4 cm) wide and thread them onto metal skewers.

Brush the meatballs with olive oil and sprinkle with salt. Place the skewers on an oiled grill rack or a broiler pan and grill or broil, turning to brown on all sides, until cooked through, about 8 minutes.

Remove the skewers from the grill or broiler and slip the meatballs off the skewers. Cut the pita breads into halves and tuck a meatball into the each half. Serve at once. Offer the yogurt sauce and onion salad at the table for guests to add to taste.

Serves 6

Braised Pork with Quinces

Quinces are prized in Greece and Turkey during the fall months, when their unique scent perfumes every kitchen. If you cannot find quinces, substitute apples or pears and reduce the sugar to 2 tablespoons. Although pork is naturally sweet and a wonderful foil for quince, this stew can also be made with beef or lamb.

2½ lb (1.25 kg) boneless pork shoulder, trimmed of excess fat and cut into 2-inch (5-cm) cubes
2 teaspoons ground cinnamon
2 teaspoons ground cumin
Juice of 1 lemon
3 lb (1.5 kg) quinces
2 tablespoons unsalted butter
½ cup (4 oz/125 g) sugar
1 cup (8 fl oz/250 ml) pomegranate juice or water
¼ cup (2 fl oz/60 ml) olive oil
2 onions, chopped
Pinch of ground cayenne pepper, optional
1 cup (8 fl oz/250 ml) chicken stock or water
Salt and freshly ground black pepper

❋ Rub the meat with 1 teaspoon each of the cinnamon and cumin. Place the spice-coated meat in a non-aluminum bowl, cover and let marinate for 2 hours at room temperature or overnight in the refrigerator.

❋ Fill a large bowl three-fourths full with water and add the lemon juice. Peel the quinces, core them and then slice thickly. As they are cut, drop them into the bowl of lemon water to prevent discoloring until all are cut.

❋ Drain the quince slices and pat dry. In a sauté pan over high heat, melt the butter. Add the quinces and sauté until softened, about 10 minutes. Sprinkle with the sugar and continue to sauté until golden, 15–20 minutes longer. Add the pomegranate juice or water and simmer over medium heat until tender, 15–20 minutes. Remove from the heat and let stand for 1 hour.

❋ Return the quinces to a simmer over medium heat and simmer for 15 minutes longer. Remove from the heat and let stand for 1 hour longer; or let cool, cover and let stand overnight.

❋ In a large, heavy sauté pan over medium heat, warm the olive oil. Add the pork and brown on all sides, about 10 minutes. Using a slotted spoon, transfer the pork to a plate and set aside.

❋ To the fat remaining in the pan, add the onions. Sauté over medium heat until tender, about 8 minutes. Add the remaining 1 teaspoon each cinnamon and cumin and the cayenne, if using. Sauté a few minutes longer to blend the flavors and then return the meat to the pan. Add the 1 cup (8 fl oz/250 ml) stock or water and stir well. Reduce the heat to low, cover and simmer for 1 hour.

❋ Place the pan holding the quinces over medium heat and bring to a simmer. Simmer for 15 minutes. Add the quinces and their juices to the meat and continue to simmer over low heat until the meat is tender and the flavors have blended, about 30 minutes longer. Season to taste with salt and pepper.

❋ Spoon the stew into a warmed serving dish and serve hot.

Serves 6

Lamb Stew with Artichokes

While artichokes are the classic choice for this dill-scented stew, you could replace them with celery, fennel or carrots. The last-minute avgolemono *thickening of egg and lemon is an added flourish that truly pulls the dish together. The stew can be prepared a day or two ahead; add the* avgolemono *during reheating.*

3–4 tablespoons olive oil

2½ lb (1.25 kg) boneless lamb shoulder, trimmed of excess fat and cut into 2-inch (5-cm) pieces

3 onions, chopped

3 cloves garlic, minced

1½ cups (12 fl oz/375 ml) water or chicken stock, or as needed

½ cup (4 fl oz/120 ml) fresh lemon juice

6 medium-sized artichokes

2 lb (1 kg) assorted greens such as romaine (cos), dandelion greens or Swiss chard (silverbeet), stemmed, well rinsed, drained and torn into bite-sized pieces (optional)

Salt

½ cup (¾ oz/20 g) chopped fresh dill

Freshly ground pepper

2 eggs, at room temperature

※ In a large sauté pan over high heat, warm 2 tablespoons of the olive oil. Working in batches, add the lamb and brown on all sides, about 10 minutes. Using a slotted spoon, transfer the browned lamb to a large, heavy pot.

※ Add more olive oil if needed to the sauté pan and then add the onions. Sauté over medium heat until softened, about 5 minutes. Add the garlic and sauté for 3 minutes longer. Transfer the contents of the sauté pan to the pot containing the lamb. Raise the heat to high, pour ½ cup (4 fl oz/125 ml) of the water or stock into the sauté pan, and deglaze the pan by stirring to dislodge any browned bits from the pan bottom. Then add the pan juices to the lamb.

※ Add the remaining 1 cup (8 fl oz/250 ml) water or stock to the pot, or as needed to cover the meat. Bring to a boil, reduce the heat to low, cover and simmer for 45 minutes.

※ Meanwhile, fill a large bowl three-fourths full with water and add ¼ cup (2 fl oz/60 ml) of the lemon juice. Snap off the tough outer leaves from the artichokes. Using a paring knife, trim the dark green parts from the base and stem. Cut the artichokes lengthwise into quarters, then scoop out and discard the prickly chokes. As they are cut, drop the artichokes into the bowl of lemon water to prevent discoloring until needed.

※ If using the greens, fill a large saucepan three-fourths full with water and bring to a boil. Add salt to taste and then the greens. Boil until tender, about 10 minutes, then drain well.

※ When the lamb has simmered for 45 minutes, drain the artichokes and add them to the pot along with the greens. Continue to simmer until the lamb and artichokes are tender, about 20 minutes longer.

※ Add the dill and season to taste with salt and pepper. Simmer for 5 minutes. At the last minute, in a bowl, beat the eggs until very frothy. Gradually beat in the remaining ¼ cup (2 fl oz/60 ml) lemon juice. Then gradually beat in about 1 cup (8 fl oz/250 ml) of the hot lamb juices, beating constantly to prevent curdling. Slowly stir the egg mixture into the hot stew. Heat through but do not allow the stew to boil.

※ Transfer to a warmed serving dish and serve hot.

Serves 4

Baked Lamb and Eggplant

This famous Greek dish is believed to have been carried to Greece by the Arabs in the Middle Ages. Moussaka *can be prepared in advance and gently reheated before serving.*

3 lb (1.5 kg) eggplants (aubergines)
   Salt

MEAT SAUCE
2 tablespoons olive oil
3 large yellow onions, chopped
2 lb (1 kg) ground (minced)
   lean lamb
3 cups (18 oz/560 g) canned
   chopped plum (Roma) tomatoes
3 tablespoons tomato paste
4 cloves garlic, finely minced
½ cup (4 fl oz/125 ml) red wine
1 tablespoon dried oregano
¾ cup (1 oz/30 g) chopped fresh
   flat-leaf (Italian) parsley
1 tablespoon ground cinnamon
   Pinch of ground cloves or allspice
   Salt and freshly ground pepper

   Olive oil for brushing

BÉCHAMEL SAUCE
3 tablespoons unsalted butter
3 tablespoons all-purpose (plain)
   flour
3 cups (24 fl oz/750 ml) hot milk
½ teaspoon freshly grated nutmeg
   Salt and freshly ground pepper
3 eggs, lightly beaten
1 cup (8 oz/250 g) whole-milk
   ricotta cheese
½ cup (2 oz/60 g) fine dried bread
   crumbs
1 cup (4 oz/125 g) freshly grated
   kefalotiri or Parmesan cheese

Peel the eggplants and cut into slices ½ inch (12 mm) thick. Place the eggplant slices in a colander, sprinkle with salt and let stand for 1 hour to drain off the bitter juices.

Meanwhile, make the meat sauce: In a large frying pan over medium heat, warm the olive oil. Add the onions and sauté until tender, about 8 minutes. Add the lamb and cook until the meat loses its redness and starts to brown, 5–7 minutes. Add the tomatoes, tomato paste, garlic, wine, oregano, parsley, cinnamon and ground cloves or allspice and simmer over low heat until thickened and most of the liquid is absorbed, about 45 minutes. If it begins to look too dry, add a little water. Taste and adjust the seasonings with salt, pepper and the spices. Set aside.

Preheat an oven to 400°F (200°C). Rinse the eggplant slices with cool water, drain well and pat dry with paper towels. Place on baking sheets, brush the tops with olive oil and bake in the oven, turning once and brushing on the second side with oil, until tender, golden and translucent, 15–20 minutes. Transfer to paper towels to drain.

To make the béchamel sauce, in a small saucepan over low heat, melt the butter. Whisk in the flour and raise the heat to medium. Cook, stirring, for 2 minutes. (Do not brown.) Gradually whisk in the hot milk and bring to a boil over high heat. Reduce the heat to medium and simmer until thickened, 2–3 minutes. Add the nutmeg, season to taste with salt and pepper and remove from the heat. In a small bowl, whisk the eggs and ricotta until well blended, then whisk into the hot sauce.

Reduce the oven temperature to 350°F (180°C).

To assemble the *moussaka,* oil an 11-by-15-inch (28-by-37.5-cm) baking dish. Sprinkle ¼ cup (1 oz/30 g) of the bread crumbs on the bottom of the dish. Arrange half of the eggplant slices in the dish and spoon the meat sauce over them. Layer the remaining eggplant slices on top and pour the béchamel evenly over the surface. Sprinkle with the remaining ¼ cup (1 oz/30 g) bread crumbs and then with the cheese.

Bake until heated through and the top is golden brown, about 45 minutes. Remove from the oven and let stand for 15 minutes before cutting into squares to serve.

Serves 8–10

Grilled Lamb on Skewers

The tantalizing aroma of grilling lamb pervades the cities of the eastern Mediterranean. In Greece, this same preparation is called arni souvlakia. *The marinade also works well on lamb chops and on butterflied leg of lamb. Serve atop eggplant and tomato pilaf (recipe on page 65) or with pita bread.*

2 small onions, grated

1 cup (8 fl oz/250 ml) olive oil

1 teaspoon freshly ground black pepper, plus ground black pepper to taste

1 teaspoon dried oregano or 2 teaspoons fresh thyme

1 teaspoon ground cinnamon

1 teaspoon ground cumin
    Pinch of ground cayenne pepper, optional

2 lb (1 kg) tender lamb from the leg, trimmed of fat and cut across the grain into 1½-inch (4-cm) cubes

1 red (Spanish) onion, cut into 1-inch (2.5-cm) squares
    Salt

2 ripe but firm tomatoes, cored and halved

2 green bell peppers (capsicums), seeded, deribbed and cut into 1½-inch (4-cm) squares
    Yogurt-cucumber sauce *(recipe on page 13)*

※ In a nonaluminum bowl, combine the onions, ¾ cup (6 fl oz/190 ml) of the olive oil, the 1 teaspoon black pepper, oregano or thyme, cinnamon, cumin and the cayenne, if using. Stir to mix well, then add the lamb cubes, turning to coat evenly. Cover and let marinate overnight in the refrigerator.

※ Prepare a fire in a charcoal grill or preheat a broiler (griller).

※ Remove the lamb cubes from the marinade, reserving the marinade, and thread them onto metal skewers, alternating them with the onion pieces. (Do not pack the lamb and onion pieces too tightly or they will not cook evenly.) Brush the lamb and onions with some of the remaining ¼ cup (2 fl oz/60 ml) olive oil and sprinkle with salt and black pepper. Thread the tomatoes and bell peppers on separate skewers, brushing them with oil and sprinkling with salt and pepper as well.

※ Place the lamb-filled skewers on an oiled grill rack or a broiler pan and grill or broil, turning once and basting occasionally with the reserved marinade, until the meat is done to your liking, 8–10 minutes total for medium-rare. About 5 minutes before the lamb is ready, add the tomato and pepper skewers to the grill rack or broiler pan. Grill or broil, turning as needed, until tender when pierced with a knife, about 5 minutes.

※ Transfer the skewers to a warmed serving dish or individual plates. Serve hot with the yogurt-cucumber sauce in a bowl on the side.

Serves 4–6

Roast Leg of Lamb with Yogurt

While yogurt is more commonly used as a tenderizing marinade for lamb kebabs, in this recipe from Crete it is mixed with cinnamon and spread on a leg of lamb during only the last 15 minutes of roasting. Surprisingly, the yogurt forms a wonderful savory crust.

1	leg of lamb on the bone, 5–6 lb (2.5–3 kg)
6	cloves garlic plus 2 teaspoons minced garlic
2	teaspoons plus 3 tablespoons chopped fresh rosemary
5	tablespoons (2½ fl oz/75 ml) olive oil
4	tablespoons (2 fl oz/60 ml) fresh lemon juice
	Salt and freshly ground pepper
1½	cups (12 oz/375 g) whole or lowfat plain yogurt
1	teaspoon ground cinnamon
½	teaspoon all-purpose (plain) flour

※ Using a small, sharp knife, cut about 12 slits, each about ½ inch (12 mm) deep, in the leg of lamb, spacing them evenly. Cut 3 of the garlic cloves into thin slivers and place in a small bowl with the 2 teaspoons rosemary. Mix well and insert the garlic mixture in the slits.

※ Finely chop the remaining 3 garlic cloves and place in a small bowl. Add 2 tablespoons of the rosemary, 2 tablespoons of the olive oil and 2 tablespoons of the lemon juice and mix well. Rub this mixture all over the leg of lamb. Cover and let marinate for 2 hours at room temperature or overnight in the refrigerator.

※ Preheat an oven to 350°F (180°C).

※ Place the lamb in a roasting pan and sprinkle with salt and pepper. In a small bowl, whisk together the remaining 3 tablespoons olive oil, the remaining 2 tablespoons lemon juice, the remaining 1 tablespoon rosemary and the 2 teaspoons minced garlic. Roast the lamb, basting every 20 minutes with the oil-lemon mixture, for 1¼ hours.

※ In another bowl, whisk together the yogurt, cinnamon and flour. Spoon the mixture over the lamb and continue to roast until the yogurt sauce sets up and the lamb is done to your liking, about 15 minutes longer for medium-rare. To test, insert an instant-read thermometer into the thickest part of the leg away from the bone; it should register 125°F (52°C) for medium-rare.

※ Transfer the lamb to a warmed serving platter and let rest for 8–10 minutes, then carve and serve hot.

Serves 6

Pork Ragout with Sweet Red Peppers and Lemon

This recipe combines the best of two classic Portuguese dishes. One sautés and then braises pork slices with sweet red peppers and white wine; the other stews cumin-and-garlic-scented pork in white wine. The aromatic result is perfectly accented with slices of lemon and chopped cilantro.

3 tablespoons cumin seeds

2 tablespoons minced garlic

1 teaspoon kosher salt

1 teaspoon freshly ground pepper

1 tablespoon paprika

2 lb (1 kg) boneless pork shoulder, cut into 1-inch (2.5-cm) cubes

¼ cup (2 oz/60 g) lard or (2 fl oz/60 ml) olive oil

4 red bell peppers (capsicums), seeded, deribbed and cut lengthwise into strips ½ inch (12 mm) wide

1 cup (8 fl oz/250 ml) dry white wine

½ cup (4 fl oz/125 ml) chicken stock

6 paper-thin lemon slices, cut into half rounds

½ cup (¾ oz/20 g) chopped fresh cilantro (fresh coriander)

❋ Put the cumin seeds in a small, dry frying pan and place over medium heat, swirling the pan occasionally, until toasted and fragrant, 2–3 minutes. Transfer to a spice grinder or peppermill and grind finely.

❋ In a mortar, combine the ground cumin, garlic, salt, pepper and paprika and mash with a pestle to form a paste. Place the pork in a nonaluminum bowl and rub the paste evenly over the meat. Cover and let marinate overnight in the refrigerator.

❋ Bring the meat to room temperature. In a large sauté pan over high heat, warm the lard or olive oil. Working in batches, add the pork and brown quickly on all sides, 5–8 minutes. Using tongs or a slotted spoon, transfer the pork to a large, heavy pot. Add the pepper strips to the fat remaining in the pan and sauté until softened, about 5 minutes.

❋ Transfer the pepper strips to the pot containing the pork. Return the sauté pan to high heat, pour the wine into the pan and deglaze the pan by stirring to dislodge any browned bits from the pan bottom. Add the pan juices to the pork and peppers. Add the stock and lemon slices and bring to a boil. Quickly reduce the heat to low, cover and simmer until the pork is very tender, about 25 minutes.

❋ Stir in the cilantro, then taste and adjust the seasonings. Spoon into a warmed serving dish and serve hot.

Serves 4–6

Desserts

If dessert is eaten in a taverna, it usually consists of little more than a wedge of cheese or a piece of perfectly ripe fruit. Because the taverna and its Mediterranean counterparts often have only the most rudimentary kitchens, any pastries that might be served are usually bought at a local shop, where the baker may make just one or two sweets along with loaves of country-style bread.

The desserts that are made at a taverna are both simple and homey—vanilla-scented rice pudding and orange-flavored baked custard are just two of the favorites one can expect to find. Cheese- or fruit-filled tartlets or cookies are also baked on occasion, but only if space and time allow.

Dried fruits and nuts are an important part of the taverna dessert repertoire, and they are used with abundance in a variety of sweets and bite-sized treats. Dried figs stuffed with almonds and chocolate make tantalizing tidbits, perfect for savoring alongside a glass of port or sweet sherry. Whole Turkish apricots are also served stuffed, but with a filling of sweet cream and a coating of thick sugar syrup. Nuts are the featured ingredient in baklava, the Greek and Turkish pastry favorite in which delicate layers of filo and chopped nuts are enveloped by a subtle lemony syrup.

Cream-Filled Apricots

Whole dried Turkish apricots work well in this dessert. When cooked, they plump up to reveal a seam where the pit was removed, which becomes a pocket for stuffing. In Turkey, a thick, clotted cream made from water buffalo's milk and known as kaymak is the prized stuffing ingredient. Italian mascarpone or French crème fraîche may be substituted.

½   lb (250 g) whole dried Turkish apricots or dried apricot halves

1½   cups (12 oz/375 g) sugar

2   cups (16 fl oz/500 ml) water

2   teaspoons fresh lemon juice

1   cup (8 fl oz/250 ml) *kaymak*, mascarpone or crème fraîche

½   cup (2 oz/60 g) chopped unsalted pistachio nuts

❋ Place the apricots in a bowl, add water to cover and let stand over-night. Drain.

❋ In a saucepan over medium heat, combine the sugar and water. Bring to a simmer, stirring to dissolve the sugar. Simmer until thickened, about 10 minutes. Add the apricots and cook until tender, about 20 minutes. Stir in the lemon juice and continue to simmer for 1 minute longer.

❋ Using a slotted spoon, transfer the apricots to a baking sheet or large plate, reserving the syrup in the pan. Let cool enough to thicken slightly. If the syrup isn't thick, reduce it a bit over medium heat.

❋ *If using whole apricots,* carefully cut each apricot along the seam with a small, sharp knife to create a pocket. Using a small spoon or a pastry bag fitted with a plain tip, spoon or pipe the *kaymak* or other filling into each pocket.

❋ *If using apricot halves,* spoon the *kaymak* or other filling onto the centers of half of them. Top with the remaining apricot halves.

❋ Arrange the apricots side by side on a serving platter. Spoon the thickened syrup over the stuffed apricots and refrigerate until the syrup is set, about 30 minutes.

❋ To serve, bring the stuffed apricots to room temperature and sprinkle with the pistachios.

Serves 4–6

Rice Pudding

Rice pudding is a popular dessert in Spain, Turkey and Greece, as well as Portugal. It is commonly made with milk, and sometimes with water. For extra tenderness, Portuguese cooks first simmer the rice in water and then add it to the milk; in Greece, the rice is cooked directly in the milk. Garnishes range from nuts and raisins to pomegranate seeds and cinnamon.

4 cups (32 fl oz/1 l) milk
⅔ cup (5 oz/155 g) sugar
1 tablespoon unsalted butter
1 lemon zest strip, about 3 inches (7.5 cm) long
1 cinnamon stick
6 cups (48 fl oz/1.5 l) water
  Pinch of salt
½ cup (3½ oz/105 g) short-grain white rice
3 egg yolks
  Ground cinnamon for garnish
  Toasted sliced (flaked) or slivered almonds for garnish, optional

In a saucepan over medium-high heat, combine the milk, sugar, butter, lemon zest and cinnamon stick. Heat until small bubbles appear along the edge of the pan, then remove from the heat. Let stand for 30 minutes to develop the flavors.

Meanwhile, in another saucepan, bring the water to a boil. Add the salt and rice, reduce the heat to low and cook slowly until the rice kernels have swelled and are tender, 15–20 minutes. Drain.

Place the saucepan holding the milk mixture over medium heat and bring to a simmer. Add the rice and simmer uncovered, stirring often, until thickened, 15–20 minutes. Remove the lemon zest and cinnamon stick and discard.

In a bowl, using a fork or whisk, beat the egg yolks until lightly frothy. Gradually add about 1 cup (8 fl oz/ 250 ml) of the hot pudding to the yolks, beating constantly. Gradually pour the warmed yolks into the remaining pudding, stirring constantly. Cook over very, very low heat, stirring constantly, for 5 minutes.

Spoon the pudding into individual dessert bowls or one large serving bowl. Sprinkle with cinnamon and top with toasted almonds, if using. Serve at room temperature.

Serves 6–8

Sweet Cheese Tarts from Santorini

Cheese tarts are enjoyed all over the Mediterranean, but are especially popular in Greece and Portugal. This particular recipe, traditionally found in the tavernas on the sun-splashed island of Santorini, produces small, delicate tartlets.

PASTRY
2   cups (8 oz/250 g) sifted all-purpose (plain) flour
¼   teaspoon salt
1   teaspoon baking powder
2   tablespoons sugar
3   tablespoons unsalted butter, at room temperature
¼   cup (2 oz/60 g) vegetable shortening
1   egg, lightly beaten
1   tablespoon water, or as needed

CHEESE FILLING
1   lb (500 g) fresh soft cheese such as mizithra, ricotta or farmer or equal parts ricotta and cream cheese
1   cup (8 oz/250 g) sugar
2   tablespoons all-purpose (plain) flour
2   egg yolks
1   teaspoon ground cinnamon, plus cinnamon for garnish, optional
    Grated orange or lemon zest, optional

※ *To make the pastry in a food processor fitted with the metal blade,* combine the flour, salt, baking powder and sugar and process briefly to mix. Add the butter and shortening and process with rapid on-off pulses until the mixture resembles coarse meal. Add the egg and the 1 tablespoon water and process to form a soft dough, adding a little more water if needed. Gather the dough together and place it on a lightly floured work surface. Knead until the dough is smooth and holds together, 5–10 minutes. Wrap in plastic wrap; refrigerate until needed.

※ *To make the pastry by hand,* combine the flour, salt, baking powder and sugar in a bowl and stir to mix. Add the butter and shortening and, using a pastry blender or 2 knives, cut them into the dry ingredients until the mixture resembles coarse meal. Add the egg and the 1 tablespoon water and, using a fork, stir together until the mixture forms a soft dough, adding a little more water if needed. Gather the dough together, then knead, shape and refrigerate as directed for the processor method.

※ To make the cheese filling, in a bowl, combine the cheese(s), sugar, flour, egg yolks, the 1 teaspoon cinnamon and the orange or lemon zest, if using. Stir to mix thoroughly.

※ Preheat an oven to 350°F (180°C).

※ Divide the dough into 12 equal balls. On a lightly floured work surface, roll out each ball into a round 4 inches (10 cm) in diameter. Carefully transfer each round to a tartlet tin 2½ inches (6 cm) in diameter, pressing the dough firmly but gently into the tin and fluting the edges. Place the pastry-lined tins on a large baking sheet. Alternatively, butter a large baking sheet. Form the 4-inch (10-cm) rounds into free-form tart shells, pinching the edges to make a fluted rim, and place on the prepared baking sheet.

※ Carefully spoon the cheese filling into the tart shells, gently smoothing the tops with a rubber spatula. Bake until the tops are a pale golden brown, 20–25 minutes.

※ Transfer to wire racks and let cool. Sprinkle with cinnamon, if using, and serve at room temperature.

Makes 12 tartlets

Figs Stuffed with Chocolate and Almonds

Although the combination might not seem obvious at first glance, one taste of these confections shows how well suited dried figs are to the rich tastes and textures of chocolate and almonds. Serve this after-dinner sweet with a glass of good Portuguese port or Madeira.

½ cup (2½ oz/75 g) slivered blanched almonds, plus 12 whole blanched almonds

¼ cup (2 oz/60 g) sugar

2 oz (60 g) semisweet chocolate, chopped

12 large dried figs

❋ Preheat an oven to 350°F (180°C).

❋ Spread the slivered and whole almonds on a baking sheet, keeping them separate. Bake until toasted and fragrant, 8–10 minutes. Let cool. Set aside the 12 whole almonds. Leave the oven set at 350°F (180°C).

❋ In a food processor fitted with the metal blade, combine the sugar, slivered almonds and chocolate. Use rapid on-off pulses to form a coarse paste.

❋ Cut off the stems from the figs. Using a small, sharp knife, cut a small slit 1 inch (2.5 cm) deep in the top of each fig. Using a small spoon, stuff each slit with about 1 teaspoon of the almond-chocolate mixture. Pinch the openings closed. As the figs are stuffed, place them on a baking sheet, stem sides up.

❋ Bake for 5 minutes. Turn the figs over and continue to bake until softened, about 5 minutes longer.

❋ Remove from the oven and press a whole almond into the slit. Serve warm or at room temperature.

Serves 6

Baklava

Both the Greeks and the Turks lay claim to this masterpiece of the Middle Eastern sweets repertoire. Baklava can be made with walnuts, almonds, hazelnuts (filberts) or pistachios or a combination of walnuts and almonds. Sticky honey syrups are never used by Greek and Turkish bakers; instead, they prepare a simple sugar syrup flavored with lemon juice and zest.

4 cups (1 lb/500 g) almonds, walnuts or equal parts almonds and walnuts, coarsely chopped
¾ cup (6 oz/185 g) sugar
1 tablespoon ground cinnamon
¼ teaspoon ground cloves
½ lb (250 g) clarified unsalted butter, melted
1 lb (500 g) filo dough, thawed in the refrigerator if frozen

LEMON SYRUP
2 cups (16 fl oz/500 ml) water
2 cups (1 lb/500 g) sugar
2 lemon zest strips, each 3 inches (7.5 cm) long
2 tablespoons fresh lemon juice

✹ Preheat an oven to 350°F (180°C).

✹ In a bowl, combine the nuts, sugar, cinnamon and cloves.

✹ Lightly brush a 9-by-14-by-2-inch (23-by-35-by-5-cm) baking pan with some of the melted butter. Remove the filo sheets from their package, lay them flat on a work surface and cover with a damp towel or plastic wrap to prevent them from drying out. Lay a filo sheet in the prepared pan and brush it lightly with butter. Working with 1 sheet at a time, top with half of the remaining filo sheets (10–12 sheets), brushing each sheet with butter after it is placed in the pan. Spread the nut mixture evenly over the stacked filo sheets. Then top with the remaining filo sheets, again brushing each sheet lightly with butter, including the top sheet. Cover and refrigerate for about 30 minutes so the butter will set. (This step makes the baklava easier to cut.)

✹ Using a sharp knife, cut the baklava all the way through into diamond shapes, forming about 36 pieces in all. Bake until golden, 35–40 minutes.

✹ While the baklava is baking, make the syrup: In a deep saucepan, combine the water, sugar and lemon zest. Bring to a boil, reduce the heat to low and simmer until thickened, about 15 minutes. Remove the lemon zest and discard. Stir in the lemon juice.

✹ When the baklava is done, remove it from the oven. Pour the hot syrup evenly over the hot pastry. Let stand for 30 minutes to cool slightly, then recut the diamonds. Serve warm or at room temperature. Store leftover pieces covered at room temperature.

Makes about 36 pieces

Caramelized Orange Custard

Flan is the most popular dessert in almost every Spanish taberna, as well as in Portuguese tascas, where a little port or orange zest is sometimes added to flavor the custard base. Usually the custard is caramelized—that is, baked in ramekins or custard cups that have been lined with caramel to create a sweet, golden sauce.

Zest of 3 oranges, in long strips
2 cups (16 fl oz/500 ml) milk
2 cups (16 fl oz/500 ml) heavy (double) cream
1 cinnamon stick
2 cups (1 lb/500 g) sugar
¼ cup (2 fl oz/60 ml) water
6 whole eggs plus 3 egg yolks
1 teaspoon vanilla extract (essence)
3 tablespoons port wine, optional

※ In a saucepan over medium-high heat, combine the orange zest, milk, cream and cinnamon stick. Heat until small bubbles appear at the edge of the pan, then remove from the heat. Let stand for 1 hour to develop the flavors.

※ In a small, heavy saucepan over low heat, combine 1 cup (8 oz/250 g) of the sugar and the water. Stir until the sugar dissolves. Bring to a boil over high heat. Boil, without stirring, until the liquid is golden brown, 6–8 minutes. Carefully pour the hot syrup into the bottoms of eight 1-cup (8–fl oz/250-ml) ramekins or custard cups, immediately tilting and swirling the dishes to coat the bottoms and sides with the caramel. Place the dishes in a large baking pan. Set aside.

※ Preheat an oven to 325°F (165°C).

※ Strain the cream mixture through a sieve into a clean saucepan. Warm over medium-high heat until tiny bubbles appear along the edge of the pan. (Do not allow to boil.)

※ Meanwhile, in a bowl, whisk together the whole eggs, egg yolks and the remaining 1 cup (8 oz/250 g)

sugar until frothy. Gradually beat in the hot cream mixture, a little at a time. Stir in the vanilla, and then the wine, if using. Strain the mixture through a sieve into the caramel-lined dishes, dividing it evenly.

※ Pour hot water into the baking pan to reach halfway up the sides of the custard cups. Cover the pan with foil and place in the oven. Bake until a knife inserted in the center of a custard comes out clean, about 30 minutes.

※ Remove the baking pan from the oven and remove the dishes from the pan. Let cool for 30 minutes, then cover and refrigerate until well chilled.

※ Just before serving, carefully run a knife around the inside edge of each custard and invert into individual shallow dessert bowls. Pour any extra caramel in the dishes over the custards and serve.

Serves 8

Glossary

The following glossary defines common ingredients and cooking procedures, as well as special cooking equipment, used in tavernas.

Bell Peppers

These sweet, bell-shaped red, yellow or green peppers, also known as capsicums, originated in the New World, but they had spread throughout the Mediterranean within a century or so of Christopher Columbus's first voyage. The seeds of bell peppers are indigestible and should be removed before the peppers are added to dishes.

Breads

To serve with authentic Mediterranean-style meals, choose a good rustic loaf made from unbleached wheat flour, with a firm, coarse crumb. For Greek and Turkish specialties, also look for Greek pita (below) or Turkish *pide,* round or oval flat pocket breads.

Butter

While olive oil predominates in Mediterranean cuisines, un-salted butter is also used for cooking. To prevent butter from burning at high baking temperatures, it should be clarified—that is, its milk solids and water content removed from the fat—before use.

TO CLARIFY BUTTER

Melt the butter in a small saucepan over very low heat. Remove from the heat and let stand briefly. Using a spoon, skim off and discard the foam from the surface. Pour off the clear yellow oil, leaving the milky solids and water behind. The clarified butter can be refrigerated for up to 1 month or frozen for 2 months.

Cheeses

Records trace the consumption of cheese in the Mediterranean as far back as the Bronze Age. Today, scores of cheeses may be found on the tables of casual restaurants everywhere in the region.

Farmer Similar in appearance to ricotta, this small-curd, cow's milk cheese is low in fat and has a fairly dry consistency.

Feta Traditional brine-cured Greek sheep's or goat's milk cheese (1).

Kasseri Greek sheep's or goat's milk cheese (3) with a semi-hard consistency similar to Cheddar, punctuated by a few tiny holes, and a taste similar to feta.

Kaymak This Turkish thickened cream is used mostly in desserts. English-style clotted cream or French crème fraîche may be substituted.

Kefalotiri Hard, yellow common Greek grating cheese (2), made from unpasteurized sheep's or goat's milk.

Mizithra A fresh cheese made from the whey produced in the making of feta or Kefalotiri cheese. Oftentimes whole fresh sheep's or cow's milk is added to enrich the final result.

Parmesan Hard, thick-crusted Italian cow's milk cheese with a sharp, salty, full flavor acquired during at least two years of aging. Buy in block form to grate fresh as needed.

Ricotta A light-textured, mild and soft fresh Italian cheese made from twice-cooked milk —traditionally sheep's milk, although cow's milk ricotta is far more common today. Sold in small tubs in most markets.

Chili Peppers

The New World's varied chili peppers, both fresh and dried, were introduced to Mediterranean kitchens soon after the first voyage of Columbus. Those used in this book include *ancho chilies,* the dried form of the ripened mild to hot poblano chili; the *jalapeño,* a small, thick-fleshed, fiery-hot green or red chili; mild to moderately hot chilies such as the blackish green *pasilla,* also known as the Chilaca chili; the long green *Anaheim,* also known as the New Mexico or simply the long green chili; and any of a variety of small, hot *red chilies* such as the serrano and jalapeño.

Currants, Dried

Produced from a small variety of grapes, these dried fruits resemble tiny raisins; but they have a stronger, tarter flavor than their larger cousins, which may be substituted for them in recipes.

Eggplant

Tender, mildly earthy, sweet vegetable-fruit covered with tough, shiny skin, which may be peeled, or left unpeeled if used in certain long-cooking dishes. Eggplants vary in color from the familiar purple to red and from yellow to white. The most common variety is the large, purple globe eggplant, but many markets also carry the slender, purple Asian eggplant, which is more tender and has fewer, smaller seeds. Also known as aubergine.

Fava Beans

Also known as broad bean and resembling an oversized lima bean, this variety spread from ancient Egypt northward into the Mediterranean. Fresh fava beans are sold in their long pods and are easily shelled. Some cooks also remove the tough but edible skin that encases each bean.

TO PREPARE FAVA BEANS
With your fingers, pop open the bean pods along their seams and pull out the individual fava beans. Use a thumbnail to split open the tough outer skin of each bean, then peel it off with your fingertips.

Filo Dough
Taking its name from the Greek word for leaf, this pastry dough consists of paper-thin sheets that are used to enfold a variety of savory and sweet dishes from the eastern Mediterranean. Also spelled *phyllo,* it may be found fresh or frozen in ethnic food stores and well-stocked markets; be sure to thaw frozen filo in the refrigerator before use. When working with filo, keep those sheets you are not handling at the moment well covered to prevent drying out.

Garlic
The Crusaders spread the use of this intensely aromatic bulb throughout the Mediterranean, where it remains a favorite seasoning. Peel cloves of their thin, papery skins before using.

Grape Leaves
In Greek and Turkish dishes, among those of other Middle Eastern countries, grapevine leaves are commonly used as edible wrappers. If fresh leaves are available, rinse them thoroughly, then blanch in boiling water for about 30 seconds before use. Bottled leaves, available in ethnic delicatessens and the specialty-food section of well-stocked food markets, should be gently rinsed of their brine before use.

Ham
Cured pork products are hallmarks of the casual country cuisines of Greece, Spain and Portugal. The two types of ham used in this book are:

Prosciutto This Italian air-cured raw ham, a specialty of Parma, has a distinctively intense, savory-sweet flavor.

Serrano Spain's answer to prosciutto, serrano ham has a somewhat tougher, chewier texture, which reflects the less-pampered pigs from which it is produced.

Herbs
Fresh and dried herbs bring their diverse flavors to the cuisines of the Mediterranean. Some common ones include:

Bay Leaf The dried leaves of the bay laurel tree give their pungent, spicy flavor to sauces and other simmered dishes.

Cilantro Green, leafy herb resembling flat-leaf (Italian) parsley, with a sharp, aromatic, somewhat astringent flavor. Popular in Latin American and Asian cuisines. Also called fresh coriander and commonly referred to as Chinese parsley.

Dill Herb with fine, feathery leaves and sweet, aromatic flavor well suited to pickling brines, vegetables, seafood, and light meats. Sold fresh or dried.

Marjoram Pungent and aromatic, this herb may be used dried or fresh to season lamb and other meats, poultry, seafood, vegetables or eggs.

Mint Refreshing herb available in many varieties, with spearmint the most common. Used fresh to flavor a variety of dishes.

Oregano Also known as wild marjoram, oregano is noted for its aromatic, spicy flavor, which intensifies with drying.

Parsley Fresh parsley is used both to flavor long-simmered dishes and as a garnish. The flat-leaf (Italian) variety (below) has a more pronounced flavor that makes it generally preferable to the curly leaf type.

Thyme This delicately fragrant, clean-tasting, small-leaved herb is used fresh—whether as whole sprigs, individual leaves or chopped—or dried to flavor savory dishes.

Kale
This rustic member of the cabbage family has long, dark green, crinkly leaves with a strong taste and sturdy texture.

Leeks
These sweet, moderately flavored members of the onion family are long and cylindrical, with a pale white root end and dark green leaves.

Mortar and Pestle
Bowl-shaped mortars—stone, marble, earthenware, metal or wood—and rod-shaped pestles are the original rustic food processors of the Mediterranean. Together they are used to grind, pulverize, crush or purée all kinds of foods, from spice seeds to cooked vegetables.

Mushrooms
Meaty in texture and rich and earthy in taste, mushrooms inspire cooks throughout the Mediterranean. In addition to the familiar cultivated *white* or *button* mushrooms and their flavorful brown cousins, known as *cremini,* there are quite a few lesser-known varieties.

Portobello mushrooms are fully matured cremini, with wide, flat, deep brown caps and a rich flavor. *Chanterelles* are mild-flavored, yellowish, trumpet-shaped mushrooms.

Nuts

Throughout the Mediterranean, nuts appear in a wide variety of savory and sweet dishes. Those in this book include:

Almonds The ancient Romans called these mellow, sweet-flavored, widely popular oval nutmeats Greek nuts, referring to the path they took from Asia to Europe. Almonds are sometimes sold blanched, that is, with their brown skins removed.

Hazelnuts Also known as filberts, hazelnuts are rich-tasting, spherical nuts.

Walnuts Mentioned in Homer's epic poems, walnuts have a rich flavor and a crisp texture. English walnuts are the most common variety.

Oils

Although olive oil is usually the first choice of cooks throughout the Mediterranean, other oils are also used.

Olive Oil Extra-virgin olive oil, extracted from olives on the first pressing without the use of heat or chemicals, is valued for its distinctive fruity flavor, which reflects the olives from which it was pressed. Virgin olive oil has a less-refined flavor but is no less pure. Products labeled pure olive oil are less aromatic and flavorful still, and may be used for general cooking purposes.

Peanut Oil This pale gold oil, subtly flavored with the peanut's richness, can be heated to fairly high temperatures for deep-frying, and may also be used for sautéing and in dressings.

Vegetable Oil The term may be applied to any of several refined pure or blended oils extracted from any of a number of sources—corn, cottonseed, peanuts, safflower seeds, soybeans, sunflower seeds. Such oils are selected for their pale color, neutral flavor and high cooking temperature.

Olives

The olive tree was a sacred symbol of ancient Athens, and olives are still prominently featured in the foods of Greece as well as in other Mediterranean countries. In all these countries, ripe black and underripe green olives are cured in various combinations of salt, seasonings, brines, oils and vinegars to produce a wide range of piquant and pungent results, notably among which are Kalamata olives from the Greek Peloponnesus.

Pine Nuts

These small, ivory-colored nuts are the seeds of the stone pine tree, a Mediterranean species, and have a rich, delicately resinous flavor.

Quince

The yellowish green fruit of a tree originating in Asia but grown throughout the Mediterranean. Resembling a lumpy pear, the quince has a hard, harshly acidic flesh that becomes delicate and sweet when cooked.

Rice

Originating in Asia, rice first reached Europe when Alexander the Great introduced it to the markets of Greece following his invasion of India in 327 B.C. Arab merchants later popularized it on the Iberian Peninsula. Among the many varieties grown throughout the world, the types called for in this book are:

Long-Grain White The most popular type of rice, with long, slender grains that steam to a light, fluffy consistency. The basmati variety, in particular, is prized for its fragrant aroma and flavor.

Short-Grain White Any of several varieties of milled rice whose grains cook up to a more starchy, sticky consistency—characteristics prized in, for example, the paella of Spain.

Salt

Coarse-grained salt is used primarily in marinades and seasonings. Kosher salt is a flaked variety of coarse-grained salt that is free of additives and often preferred for cooking.

Salt Cod

Throughout the Mediterranean, and particularly in Portugal, Spain and France, codfish that has been preserved by salting and drying has been a basic food for centuries. Before cooking, salt cod must be reconstituted and rid of some of its saltiness by soaking.

Sausages

In tavernas, fresh and dried sausages may be served as simple appetizers or used as an ingredient in robust dishes. The sausages called for in this book include:

Chouriço The cured pork sausage of Portugal, flavored with a combination of garlic, paprika, salt, and other spices.

Chorizo The cured pork sausage of Spain, mildly spiced but still robustly flavored with paprika and garlic.

Italian Sweet Sausages The fresh pork sausages of northern Italy are generally sweet and mild in flavor, and sometimes flavored with fennel seed.

Linguiça A type of *chouriço,* this Portuguese dried sausage has a distinctive garlicky flavor.

Loukanika Fresh Greek pork sausage traditionally flavored with orange zest, marjoram, coriander and allspice.

Shellfish

Shellfish are popular in taverna dishes. Some varieties include:

Clams This grayish tan bivalve is much used in the dishes of Spain and Portugal. For appetizers and dishes such as paella, seek out small, sweet clams such as the Manila variety.

Mussels These common bivalves must be cleaned before cooking to remove any dirt caked on their bluish black shells and to remove their "beards," the fibrous threads by which they connect to rocks or piers in the coastal waters where they live.

Shrimp Raw shrimp (prawns) are generally sold with the heads already removed but the shells still intact. Before cooking, they are usually peeled and their thin, veinlike intestinal tracts removed.

TO PEEL AND DEVEIN

Use your thumbs to split open the thin shell between the legs, peeling it away. With a small, sharp knife, make a shallow slit along the back to expose the veinlike, usually dark intestinal tract; lift it up and pull it out.

Spices

For the best flavor, grind whole spices with a mortar and pestle or in a spice grinder just before use.

Allspice This sweet spice has a flavor reminiscent of a blend of cinnamon, cloves and nutmeg. It may be purchased as whole dried berries or ground.

Cayenne Pepper Very hot ground spice derived from the dried cayenne chili pepper.

Cinnamon The aromatic bark of a type of evergreen tree, this popular sweet spice traditionally flavors baked goods, and also finds its way into savory dishes in Greek and Turkish kitchens. It is sold as whole dried strips about 3 inches (7.5 cm) long—cinnamon sticks—or ground.

Cumin This pungent, yellowish brown spice, native to the Middle East, has a dusky, aromatic flavor. Sold ground or as crescent-shaped seeds.

Nutmeg A sweet spice derived from the hard pit of the nutmeg tree's fruit. Sold ground or whole to be grated fresh as needed.

Paprika Reddish ground spice derived from the sweet (mild) and hot forms of the dried paprika pepper.

Red Pepper Flakes Coarsely ground flakes of dried red chilies, including seeds, which add mildly hot flavor to recipes.

Saffron Threads This intensely aromatic, golden orange spice, made from the dried stigmas of a species of crocus, is sold either as threads—the dried stigmas—or in powdered form. Look for products labeled pure saffron.

Sumac Sour in taste, with overtones of lemon and pepper, this purple powder is derived from the dried berries, and sometimes the leaves, of a nonpoisonous Turkish species of the sumac shrub.

Tomatoes

During the peak of the tomato season in summer, use the best sun-ripened tomatoes you can find. At other times of the year, plum tomatoes, sometimes called Roma or egg tomatoes, will most likely have the best flavor and texture. In cooked dishes, intense tomato flavor is often derived from tomato paste, a commercial concentrate of puréed tomatoes added in small quantities to recipes.

Zucchini

These cylindrical green New World squashes enjoy widespread popularity in Mediterranean kitchens. Seek out smaller zucchini, which have a finer texture and tinier seeds. Also known as courgettes.

ACKNOWLEDGMENTS

Joyce Goldstein extends her thanks to the staff at Square One. She would also like to thank Sharon Silva for her superb editing, as well as Wendely Harvey and Lisa Atwood. Much appreciation also goes to those at Oldways Preservation and Exchange Trust—Dun Gifford, Greg Drescher and Sara Baer-Sinnott—for allowing her to reexperience firsthand the wonderful cuisine of Greece, Turkey and Spain.

❧

For lending photographic props, the photographer and stylist would like to thank:

Kim Kineman,
Woollahra, NSW

Art of Food and Wine,
Woollahra, NSW

Accoutrement,
Mosman, NSW

❧

For their valuable editorial support, the publishers would like to thank:
Desne Border, Erkan Gözüm, Ken DellaPenta and Tina Schmitz.

❧

Index

Almonds
   baklava 120
   figs stuffed with chocolate and 119
   fried 11
   sauce 79
Apricots, cream-filled 112
Artichokes
   city-style braised 61
   lamb stew with 100

Baklava 120
Béchamel sauce 103
Beef
   grilled meatballs 96
   meatball soup with egg and lemon 50
Beverages 10–11
Bread soup with cilantro, garlic and poached egg 45
Butter, clarifying 124

Cheese
   -filled pastries 37
   fried 29
   spinach filo pie 38
   tarts, sweet 116
   varieties of 124
Chicken
   with eggplant, peppers and tomatoes 91
   kebabs, grilled 88
   paella 84
   roast, with oregano and lemon 92
Chili pepper sauce 15
City-style braised artichokes 61
Clams
   paella 84
   stewed, with sausage, ham and tomatoes 68
Coffee 11
Cucumber-yogurt sauce 13
Custard, caramelized orange 123

Eggplant
   and tomato pilaf 65
   baked lamb and 103
   chicken with peppers, tomatoes and 91
   salad, grilled 33
   stuffed 58
Eggs
   caramelized orange custard 123
   meatball soup with lemon and 50
   potato omelet 22

Fava beans, preparing 125
Figs stuffed with chocolate and almonds 119
Filo dough
   baklava 120
   spinach filo pie 38
Fish
   in almond sauce 79
   in grape leaves 72
   gratin of salt cod and potatoes 75
   grilled swordfish kebabs 76
   salt cod fritters 25
   soup 49
   trout wrapped in ham 83
Fritters
   salt cod 25
   zucchini 21

Garlic
   -potato sauce 12
   sautéed mushrooms with 57
   shrimp 18
Grape leaves
   fish in 72
   stuffed 26
Gratin of salt cod and potatoes 75
Greek salad 53
"Green" soup with kale and potatoes 46

Ham
   stewed clams with sausage, tomatoes and 68
   trout wrapped in 83

Kale, "green" soup with potatoes and 46
Kebabs
   grilled chicken 88
   grilled lamb 104
   grilled swordfish 76

Lamb
   baked, and eggplant 103
   grilled, on skewers 104
   grilled meatballs 96
   meatball soup with egg and lemon 50
   pizza 34
   roast leg of, with yogurt 107
   stew with artichokes 100
Meatballs
   grilled 96
   soup with egg and lemon 50

Mushrooms, sautéed, with garlic 57
Mussels
   fish soup 49
   fried, with nut sauce 30
   paella 84

Olives, marinated 15
Omelet, potato 22
Orange custard, caramelized 123

Paella 84
Peppers
   and sausage ragout 95
   chicken with eggplant, tomatoes and 91
   chili pepper sauce 15
   pork ragout with lemon and 108
Pilafs
   eggplant and tomato 65
   paella 84
   with pine nuts and currants 62
Pizza, lamb 34
Pork. See also Ham; Sausage
   braised, with quinces 99
   ragout with sweet red peppers and lemon 108
Potatoes
   garlic-potato sauce 12
   gratin of salt cod and 75
   "green" soup with kale and 46
   omelet 22
   salt cod fritters 25

Quinces, braised pork with 99

Rice
   eggplant and tomato pilaf 65
   paella 84
   pilaf with pine nuts and currants 62
   pudding 115
   stuffed grape leaves 26
   varieties of 126

Salads
   Greek 53
   grilled eggplant 33
Salt cod
   fritters 25
   gratin of, and potatoes 75
Sauces
   almond 79
   béchamel 103

chili pepper 15
garlic-potato 12
meat 103
tomato-nut 14
yogurt 96
yogurt-cucumber 13
Sausage
   and green pepper ragout 95
   paella 84
   stewed clams with ham, tomatoes and 68
   varieties of 126
Shrimp
   fish soup 49
   garlic 18
   paella 84
   peeling and deveining 127
   with tomatoes, oregano and feta 71
Soups
   bread, with cilantro, garlic and poached egg 45
   chilled tomato 42
   fish 49
   "green," with kale and potatoes 46
   meatball, with egg and lemon 50
Spinach
   filo pie 38
   with raisins and pine nuts 54
Squid, stuffed 80

Taverna
   characteristics of 8–9
   history of 8
Tomatoes
   and eggplant pilaf 65
   chicken with eggplant, peppers and 91
   chilled tomato soup 42
   shrimp with oregano, feta and 71
   stewed clams with sausage, ham and 68
   tomato-nut sauce 14
Trout wrapped in ham 83

Yogurt
   -cucumber sauce 13
   roast leg of lamb with 107
   sauce 96

Zucchini fritters 21